MW01253099

INCARCERATING WHITE-COLLAR OFFENDERS

ABOUT THE AUTHOR

Brian K. Payne received his Ph.D. in Criminology from Indiana University of Pennsylvania in 1993. He is currently an associate professor in the Department of Sociology and Criminal Justice at Old Dominion University. He has published over thirty-five articles in scholarly journals on topics such as elder abuse, white-collar crime, and methods of social control. He is the author of *Crime and Elder Abuse: An Integrated Perspective* and coauthor of *Family Violence and Criminal Justice: A Life Course Approach.* He is a member of the Virginia Coalition for the Prevention of Elder Abuse and the National Committee for the Prevention of Elder Abuse.

INCARCERATING WHITE-COLLAR OFFENDERS

The Prison Experience and Beyond

By

BRIAN K. PAYNE, Ph.D.

Department of Sociology and Criminal Justice
Old Dominion University
Norfolk, Virginia

CHARLES C THOMAS • PUBLISHER, LTD.
Springfield • Illinois • U.S.A.

Published and Distributed Throughout the World by

CHARLES C THOMAS • PUBLISHER, LTD.
2600 South First Street
Springfield, Illinois 62704

ISBN 0-398-07344-9 (hard)
ISBN 0-398-07345-7 (paper)

Library of Congress Catalog Card Number: 2002020461

Printed in the United States of America
RR-R-3

Library of Congress Cataloging-in-Publication Data

Payne, Brian K.
    Incarcerating white-collar offenders: the prison experience and beyond/by Brian K.
Payne.
    p. cm.
    Includes bibliographical references and index.
    ISBN 0-398-07344-9 (hard) – ISBN 0-398-07345-7 (pbk.)
    1. White collar crimes. 2. Punishment. 3. Imprisonment. 4. Criminal justice,
Administration of. I.Title.

HV6768.I39 2002
364.16'8–dc21

                                                                    2002020461

Dedicated to Kathleen and Chloe

FOREWORD

Television shows such as "CSI" (crime scene investigators) and "COPS" provide good visuals. If there were such a show as "FOA" (Follow the Auditor), I doubt that it would generate the same excitement. It is easy for us as academics and media writers to focus on the episodic "crime waves" associated with the street criminal. We see muggers and burglars prey on other private citizens. Because we see ourselves primarily as individuals, and when many individuals "go bad"–a street crime wave–we believe they are collectively harming our social fabric. Legislators feel aware, knowledgeable, and comfortable when they enhance law enforcement and prosecution resources and efforts to combat individual street crime. As citizens we feel safer when we hear about increases in the severity of punishment through longer sentences and the construction of penal institutions with higher levels of security (maxi-maxi prisons). When legislators, criminal justice professionals, or citizens focus on the individual criminal, strategies for protecting ourselves from these "street criminals" follow a fairly predictable set of responses.

White-collar crime is not so simple. As the new millennium begins, the Enron scandal draws public attention to a seemingly continuous crime wave that hardly ever receives any public attention. Public discussions of Enron in various legislative and investigative Congressional committees and on various "business" television channels have betrayed a confusion and unease in dealing with the "white-collar crime waves" that may be reflection less of individuals "gone bad" than of a continuing "way of doing business." Faith in the "truthfulness" and "accuracy" and "accountability" on which the corporate–capitalist–system rely, and which Enron threatens to erode, is a true component of the social fabric.

Harm resulting from breaches of this public trust and faith is truly

vii

a social harm having effects far beyond that of the actions of any individual street criminal. In an individualistic society we are comfortable and used to discussing the individual crime and punishment that the street criminal represents. However, when it comes to crimes and practices associated with life in the offices of corporations and boardrooms, we are less aware, less knowledgeable, less comfortable and, unfortunately, less concerned.

Throughout *Incarcerating White-Collar Offenders: The Prison Experience and Beyond,* we confront the substance of white-collar crime, the thinking of white-collar criminals, and our criminological understanding of them. Here we come face to face with white-collar criminals and their motivations. Here we see that the forms of language white-collar criminals use to explain their action is more in tune with the language of the legislators, criminal justice professionals, lawyers, and academics. This makes them seem more like "one of us." And we are often less harsh in judging the behaviors of people like us. However, on further reflection, the substance of language of the white-collar criminal Payne provides lets us see the similarity with the street criminal who is normally placed outside and marginalized from us "good members" of society.

Brian Payne explores the reactions and interactions of various segments of the criminal justice system: prosecutors, courts, prisons, and community supervision, to the white-collar criminal. In exploring these reactions we begin to see the difficulties and philosophical quandaries associated with our feelings toward and responses to "upper-class" criminals. In putting all of these perspectives together, Payne gives us an opportunity to understand white-collar crime, criminals, and the punishments they receive systematically. By providing this breadth of coverage, *Incarcerating White-Collar Offenders: The Prison Experience and Beyond* gives students, teachers, and scholars an opportunity to engage in the comparative study of how we understand and react to street crime and white-collar crime.

Brian Payne's *Incarcerating White-Collar Offenders: The Prison Experience and Beyond* is also a timely book. As the millennium starts we see the growth of a global economy with open trade policies and the prospect of multinational corporations seemingly gaining primacy over nation–state governments. As these developments proceed, it is more important than ever that we develop frameworks and baseline data to access and understand unintended consequences and social harm (crime) that is likely to be produced. It is also important that we think about the impacts on motivations and the opportunities provided for potential white-collar criminals by the structures and rules that support the global business environment. It is also essential that we start to plan for the complex investigation, prosecution, and correction of the new era of white-collar crimes likely to emerge. Dr. Payne's review of our knowledge base in these areas is a good place to start.

Lucien X. Lombardo
Old Dominion University
March 6, 2002

PREFACE

White-collar crime has been a focus of a great deal of attention since Edwin Sutherland first created this concept over 60 years ago. Most of the recent attention has focused on the types of white-collar offending and the explanations for this misconduct. Much less research has considered the way the justice system responds to white-collar crime. Specifically, the incarceration experience of white-collar offenders has, with the exception of research by one scholar and his associates (see Benson, 1982; Benson & Cullen, 1988; Benson & Moore, 1992), been virtually ignored. This book fills that void in the literature by considering the way white-collar offenders experience incarceration, strategies for effectively managing institutionalized white-collar offenders, and implications for supervising white-collar offenders in the community.

In reading this book, it is my intent that four themes come across. First, white-collar crime is massive in its consequences. I finished this book right around the same time that the Enron collapse occurred. As I watched the Congressional hearings where Enron executives testified about their role, or lack of role, in the collapse, I was reminded of the fact that the response to white-collar misconduct is truly different from the response to street offenses. Imagine a Congressional hearing to determine whether drug offenders had done anything wrong. Whether the Enron collapse was due to criminal misconduct remains to be seen. What is clear is that our political system tends to afford opportunities to some white-collar offenders that are not afforded to street criminals.

Second, when I discuss ways that white-collar offenders experience punishment differently than street offenders, it is not my intent to suggest that they should be given preferential treatment. Instead, my aim is to illustrate that one size does not fit all insofar as correctional supervision is concerned. Different supervision strategies for white-collar offenders may be needed to ensure the efficiency and safety of institutional routines.

Third, I do not believe that white-collar offenders who are sentenced to prison or jail are getting off lightly. One often hears comments about white-collar offenders being sentenced to prison for too short of a time, or to prisons that are supposedly akin to paradise. There is no such thing as a nice prison for white-collar offenders. It is imperative that individuals understand that all types of prisons, from minimum security to "super max" prisons, are places that separate individuals from society. As such, the separation from society is meant to be the punishment, not the events occurring in prison.

Try a simple exercise. Think of a vacation you took where you just couldn't wait to get away from your job, home, and responsibilities. Now think of how much you looked forward to getting back to your normal routine at the end of the vacation. Imagine being stuck on that vacation for an extended period of time without any control over the time that your vacation ends. Does that sound like a vacation you want to take?

Fourth, simply because I see incarceration as a severe type of punishment for white-collar offenders does not mean that I am some bleeding heart liberal who doesn't support institutionalization of white-collar offenders. I believe that sanctions given to white-collar offenders should be proportionate to sanctions given to street offenders who committed similar offenses. Within this punitive framework, however, the justice system could do a better job in meeting the needs of individual victims and the community by focusing on ways to restore the community rather than simply looking for ways to harm offenders.

This book is intended for criminal justice professionals, academics, and researchers who want to better understand the role of the criminal justice system in punishing all types of offenders. It is also intended for use in criminal justice, corrections, sociology, and white-collar-crime courses exploring the punishment of elite offenders. Through promoting understanding about this aspect of the response to white-collar misconduct, what is needed to improve the whole justice system's response to these offenses will become evident.

ACKNOWLEDGMENTS

I am indebted to many persons whose input, insight, and assistance made this book possible. My colleagues Randy Gainey and James Oleson (each from Old Dominion University) and Tammy King (Youngstown State University) read various parts of this manuscript and encouraged me to open my mind to various aspects of the incarceration experience. I am grateful to Lou Lombardo for his words of wisdom throughout this project as well as his willingness to write the foreword of this manuscript.

I also owe my appreciation to Michael Thomas and his staff at Charles C Thomas for their guidance and faith in this project. Their prompt attention to my needs made this task easier while their professionalism made it enjoyable.

My graduate assistants, Laura Burke Fletcher and Mahmuda Khatun, helped gather and verify references, and I am thankful to them for taking on those arduous tasks. Thanks to my wife Kathleen for taking the cover photograph. Thanks also to Doug Gardner for donating his time to pose for the photo. For Ian and Bray's sake, I hope this is the only picture they ever see of their dad in handcuffs.

In addition, I am most grateful to the staff of Old Dominion University's Interlibrary Loan Department for their assistance, and for not hiding when they saw me coming. Libby Monk Turner (Chair of ODU's Department of Sociology and Criminal Justice) and Janet Katz (Acting Dean of ODU's College of Arts and Letters) also offered various types of support, for which I am thankful, to help me finish this book.

I would like to thank my extended family (including my Mom, Dad, Kim, Jack, Pam, Tyler, Kelsey, Vonda, Charlie, Heather, and Kyle) for their interest in my research. Finally, I am indebted to Kathleen and Chloe for the selfless encouragement they gave me throughout this project.

CONTENTS

INCARCERATING WHITE-COLLAR OFFENDERS

Chapter 1

WHITE-COLLAR CRIME AND WHITE-COLLAR TIME

INTRODUCTION

A tough judge nicknamed Iron Mike for his stiff sentences once stated the following in imposing a white-collar criminal's sentence: "We must shed ourselves of the perception that white-collar criminals are 'good guys' who are too good to be in jail" (Coleman, 1996: 1). Not long after this admonishment, the same judge pleaded guilty to tax evasion, was forced to quit his job, and was sent to prison for two months. In a similar case, a judge was sentenced to thirteen months in a medium security prison in which he met many individuals who were previously in his court. Some of the offenders with whom he was incarcerated actually had legal papers with the judge's name on it (McCarthy, 1996). Imagine how tough it would be to serve time with inmates whose sentences you imposed. Certainly, the protection of at-risk incarcerated white-collar criminals is one of the serious challenges jail and prison administrators face.

During the summer of 2000, 68-year-old Jai Coehlo was jailed in Rio de Janeiro pending the outcome of fraud and racketeering charges filed against him. What makes his case especially interesting is the nature of the charges. In particular, it was alleged that Coehlo, whose company supplied all prison food in Rio de Janeiro, committed fraudulent activities in fulfilling his contract to feed the prisoners covered under the contract. Reportedly, prison officials and prisoners alike complained about the horrible quality of the food. To protect the "fraudulent food man" from the inmates he had previously starved, Coehlo was segregated with older offenders who were not considered violent (Reuters, 2000).

A number of highly profiled white-collar crime cases resulting in incarceration have been the focus of a great deal of media attention. Consider, for instance, the following cases:

- In November 1990, Michael Milken was sentenced to ten years in prison and ordered to pay $600 million in restitution and fines for fraudulent securities trading, conspiracy, and the junk bond operations he oversaw.
- In October 1989, Jim Bakker was sentenced to 45 years in prison and given a $500,000 fine after the evangelist defrauded his followers by diverting over $3.7 million from his ministry.
- Jake Butcher, former chairperson of United American Bank was sentenced to 20 years in prison after he plead guilty to fraud, income tax evasion, and conspiracy (Cohen, 1990).

Other "celebrity" white-collar inmates include G. Gordon Liddy, Jeb Magruder, former Illinois Governor Dan Walker, former Louisiana Governor Edwin Edwards, and a host of others. Along with these famous offenders, thousands of other senators, preachers, governors, doctors, and members of just about every profession imaginable have been imprisoned for misdeeds committed on the job.

However, because of difficulties defining white-collar crime and detecting these offenses, no one really knows precisely how many white-collar criminals there are. Even so, the 1980s and 1990s witnessed a significant increase in the number of white-collar offenders being sentenced to jail or prison, with the majority incarcerated in federal prisons though some are incarcerated in local jails and state prisons. As Thompson (1991: 6) notes, prior to the 1980s, white-collar offenders asked, "Can I avoid prison?" Today, white-collar offenders are asking, "Can I get the top bunk?" Reasons for this increase will be considered later in this chapter. What is important at this point to establish is that very little attention has been given to what happens to white-collar offenders once they are incarcerated. Perhaps partly because there are few incarcerated white-collar offenders (as compared to incarcerated conventional offenders) and because society has generally taken an apathetic view toward incarcerated offenders (out of sight, out of mind), the experiences of white-collar offenders once they are incarcerated are not well understood. In fact, a number of myths about white-collar crime limit the ability of criminal justice professionals to effectively manage and supervise white-collar offenders. A review of eight myths will shed some light on the need to understand the way incarceration is experienced by white-collar offenders.

MYTHS ABOUT WHITE-COLLAR CRIME

Myth #1–White-collar crime is not that serious. A common assumption held by some members of the public, criminal justice officials, and legislators is that white-collar crime is not a serious problem in our society (Cullen et al., 1985). The basis for this belief is that there is often no visible physical or economic harm from white-collar offenses. The fact of the matter is, however, that the consequences of white-collar offenses are equally severe to, if not more severe than, street crimes. In the 1980s, 650 savings and loans failed, most due to fraud, costing society $500 billion (Farnham, 1990). Twelve billion a year is lost to employee theft in retail settings (Krueger, 1999). When all companies are combined, the average company loses six percent of its annual revenues to employee fraud. This amounts to a national loss of $400 billion a year (Conley, 2000).

To further understand the seriousness of the problem, consider the following:

- The average firm in one study lost $200,000 a year to fraud.
- In the same study, 76 percent of firms reported experiencing fraud in the previous year.
- Fraud in corporate America by employees costs $100 billion a year.
- Offenders steal an average of $400,000 in the typical financial statements case.
- Offenders steal an average of $102,000 in the average corruption case.
- The median loss caused by white-collar crimes is $81,500 (Conley, 2000; Sayre, 1998; Touby, 1994).

In contrast, consider the average amount lost in different types of robberies:

- The average street/highway robbery entails losses of $856.
- The average gas station robbery entails losses of $620.
- The average convenience store robbery entails losses of $627 (*Crime in the United States*, 2001).

Based on these enormous losses to white-collar crime, it should not be surprising that a recent survey by Pinkerton Security found white-collar crime to be one of the "top security threats facing corporate America" (Conley, 2000: 14).

Part of the reason for the large monetary losses to white-collar crime is due to the fact that thousands of victims can be ripped off in just one white-collar scheme. One fraudulent investor stole from 7,000 clients on his own, netting $47 million. In another case, a telemarketing ring bilked millions of dollars from 12,000 victims (Ettore, 1994; Rivera, 1998). Despite the fact that clear losses stem from these offenses, some criminal justice officials refuse to see white-collar offenses as serious. Said one judge: "[Embezzling] money is obviously different than hitting someone over the head with a pipe and robbing him. Is there societal harm done [in embezzlements]? Yes. Is it the same type of societal harm as a shooting? No" (Locy, 1998: n.p.). Locy notes that the reluctance of some officials to take white-collar crime seriously has led some experts to refer to white-collar crime as the "step-child" of the criminal justice system. This refusal to see white-collar crime as serious likely stems from a misunderstanding about the violent nature of white-collar crime. This relates to a second myth.

Myth #2−White-collar crimes are not violent crimes. Edwin Sutherland is credited with introducing the concept of white-collar crime in 1939. Sutherland (1940: 1) defined white-collar crime as "a crime committed by a person of respectability and high social status in the course of his occupation." Since then, various terms and definitions have evolved out of this definition and there has been a great deal of debate concerning the most appropriate way to define this rather broad concept. A common theme among these various concepts (e.g., occupational crime, corporate crime, elite crime, elite deviance, etc.) and definitions is that white-collar crime generally entails illegal acts of an economic nature committed during the course of employment. Defining white-collar crime by its economic costs has resulted in the actual physical or violent consequences of white-collar crime being masked.

Clearly, white-collar offenses can have serious physical consequences. David Friedrichs (1996), author of *Trusted Criminals: White-Collar Crime in Contemporary Society*, outlined a typology focusing specifically on the violent nature of many white-collar offenses. Generally referred to as corporate violence, Friedrichs explained that unsafe environmental practices (e.g., toxic waste, air pollution, and corporate destruction of a community) and unsafe products (e.g., food products, drugs, medical devices, and transportation products) can have serious devastating physical consequences for both employees of criminal corporations and consumers.

In a more immediate sense, it is also important to stress that just about any white-collar offense can result in physical harm for victims. As an illustration, in one case an 84-year-old woman and her husband lost nearly half a million dollars to a bogus investment scheme. When they learned of the fraud, the husband died of a heart attack (Galvin, 2000). In a similar case, an 81-year-old woman suffered a nervous breakdown when she learned that she had been defrauded of her life savings. Her husband suffered significant health decline as a result of the financial worries and suffered a fatal stroke (Ruth, 2000).

Although many officials do not recognize the violent nature of these offenses, victims certainly do. After losing his entire savings ($225,000) to a fraudulent investment scheme, one victim commented: "I was raped. . . . That was my kid's college money. Today, I don't trust anybody for anything" (Behar, 1998: 22). The very nature of many white-collar offenses makes the consequences similar to those experienced in violent crimes such as assault and robbery. In fact, some have argued that many types of white-collar crimes are actually worse than violent offenses for one main reason— white-collar crimes are planned, and many violent offenses are not planned (Harris & Benson, 1999). Many violent offenses occur quickly with little forethought given.

White-collar offenses, on the other hand, are usually calculated offenses that offenders plan and think about over an extended period of time before committing. Consider a case where a woman stole $100,000 from a youth hockey league over two years. The prosecutor told the judge that the offender was a "stone-cold crook." Of her offenses, the prosecutor said, "These were cold, calculated ways of taking money. . . . She stole from kids to keep her business up and running" (Pankratz, 2000: B02). The typical white-collar offender does not see his or her actions as harmful. Consequently, it is important that criminal justice officials, correctional officials in particular, recognize the harmful consequences of the crimes so that they are able to demonstrate the harmful nature of the offenses to white-collar offenders who are truly willing to change their ways. When consequences are understated, offenders are able to deny the importance of their offenses, logically making it more difficult to persuade them to change their ways. In short, if they don't think they did anything wrong, why would they change their behavior in the future? The importance of understanding consequences so that offenders can be helped is expanded in Chapter 3. At this point, a related myth is noteworthy.

Myth #3—White-collar criminals commit their offenses because they are greedy. When individuals hear of some white-collar offender stealing hundreds of thousands of dollars, a common response is to assume that some form of greed caused that offender to transgress. Although greed may indeed explain some white-collar offenses, in no way whatsoever does greed explain all types of white-collar offenses. Many people are greedy, but everyone who is greedy does not automatically commit white-collar crime. In short, the greed explanation oversimplifies the actual cause of white-collar crime.

It is important that criminal justice officials identify what they believe the causes of white-collar crime to be. Their beliefs about causality will influence how they respond to offenses, whether they are white-collar offenses or any other offense for that matter. When the causes of white-collar crime are oversimplified or misunderstood, the most effective ways to prevent future offenses are also oversimplified and misunderstood. With white-collar crime, it is important to recognize that there are several potential and overlapping factors that play a role in contributing to offenders' misdeeds.

Those factors contributing to white-collar crime include financial problems, family crises, drug addiction, gambling addiction, opportunity, fear of failure, and foolish business transactions (Benson & Moore, 1992; Breed, 1979; Locy, 1998). One manager of a federal prison unit describes white-collar offenders in his unit as "business-men who took the wrong shortcuts" (Semerad, 1998: A1). Because they are, in fact, businesspeople, their reasons for committing offenses, in many cases, may be different from reasons other offend-ers commit criminal acts. Unfortunately, it is difficult, if not impossi-ble, to determine the precise cause of most offenses. Some have likened the search for the cause of different types of crime to the search for the Holy Grail (Quinn & Tomita, 1997). The potential causes of white-collar crime are considered in more detail in the next chapter.

Myth #4–All white-collar criminals are alike. Another mis-guided assumption that individuals have about white-collar crimi-nals is that they are all alike. Just as street criminals vary in drastic ways from one another, white-collar criminals vary from one anoth-er in distinct ways as well. A church leader who defrauds his or her church members of their donations is different from a civic league treasurer who steals from the treasury. A doctor who bills Medicaid for services never provided is different from a mechanic who bills for changing your turning-signal fluid. A pharmacist who steals drugs is different from a nurse who steals drugs. A postal carrier who steals credit cards from the mail is different from a part-time cashier who steals credit card numbers at a retail store.

It is important to realize that there is significant variation among white-collar offenders. Many have a solid education though some had significant adjustment problems in high school. Some tend to be overly involved in criminal activity while others have only rarely transgressed (Benson & Moore, 1992). Weisburd et al. (1991) use the phrase "opportunity seekers" to describe those with few arrests and the phrase "deviance seekers" to describe those white-collar offend-ers who fit the conventional criminal stereotype. However, although there is enormous variation in the types of white-collar offenders, as a group, white-collar offenders are different from what are referred to by many as street criminals, common criminals, or blue-collar criminals.

Myth #5–White-collar criminals are no different than street criminals. There are also those who believe that all criminals are the same and that there are no important differences between white-collar criminals and street criminals. The evidence suggests that there are a number of differences between the two broader types of offenders. That there are differences between the two groups does not suggest that one group is "better" or "worse" than the other, nor does it suggest that one group should receive preferential treatment from correctional officials. Rather, it suggests that different strategies may be more effective for managing, supervising, and treating different types of offenders.

Generally speaking, researchers have suggested that white-collar offenders are more likely than conventional offenders to:

- Be older
- Have little previous involvement with the justice system
- Have committed property offenses
- Specialize in white-collar offenses rather than commit an assortment of offenses like street criminals do
- Be better educated
- Be from a higher social status
- Have had few problems adjusting in school
- Be free from drug problems (Benson & Cullen, 1988; Benson & Moore, 1992; Breed, 1979; Balsmeier & Kelly, 1996; Moss, 1995; Wright, 2001).

These differences between the two groups of offenders translates into the need to use different types of responses for different kinds of offenders.

For instance, sometimes arrangements must be made for certain white-collar offenders who are older with health problems (Wright, 2001). The main difference between the older white-collar offender and the older conventional offender is that the older white-collar offender has virtually no prior contact with the correctional system whereas the older conventional offender may have actually aged in prison. Because white-collar offenders begin their criminal careers at a much higher age than conventional offenders (Weisburd et al., 1990), it is conceivable that white-collar offenders are more likely than conventional offenders to enter jail or prison as husbands or wives with sons and daughters. Alternatively, younger conventional offenders are more likely to enter jail or prison as sons and daughters, but not necessarily as spouses or parents (Breed, 1979).

In a similar vein, because most white-collar offenders already have high school diplomas, educational programs offering high school diplomas or general education diplomas serve no purpose for white-collar offenders (Nadler, 1992). Rather than getting an education from the correctional system, many white-collar inmates are often proud that they can help "prison administration by utilizing their special skills" (Benson & Cullen, 1988:213).

In addition to demographic differences between the two groups, Bayse (1995) has considered the similarities and differences between the two groups' personality characteristics (see Table 1.1). As shown in Table 1.1, Bayse believes that both white-collar and conventional offenders hide behind a criminal mask, are self-centered, need power and control, lead a lifestyle of lying, and lack empathy. Alternatively, conventional offenders are more likely than street offenders to exhibit antisocial behavior, have a low frustration tolerance, use physical violence and anger as a means to an end, and have distorted ideas about love. White-collar offenders, research suggests, generally show little remorse and deny their guilt.

TABLE 1.1
PERSONALITY TRAITS OF WHITE-COLLAR OFFENDERS AND CONVENTIONAL OFFENDERS

Trait	White-Collar Offender	Conventional Offender
Criminal mask	+	+
Self-centered	+	+
Power and control oriented	+	+
Lifestyle of lying	+	+
Antisocial behavior	–	+
Low frustration tolerance	–	+
Distorted ideas about love	–	+
Violence and anger responses	–	+
Lack of remorse	+	+/–
Denials and rationalizations precipitate behavior	+	+/–
Rational offenders	+	+/–

Key:
+ means this is a common characteristic of this group.
–means this is not a common characteristic of this group.
+/– means that offenders in this group are split concerning this characteristic.

Source: Adapted from Bayse (1995).

Myth #6–No useful purpose comes from incarcerating white-collar offenders. Some individuals oppose the imprisonment of white-collar offenders because they believe that prison is too costly for nonviolent offenders who could be in the free world earning money to pay back their victims (Lott, 1990). It might be more appropriate to describe this as a controversial issue rather than a myth because a significant number of individuals will always believe that no useful purposes come from the imprisonment of nondangerous offenders–whether they are white-collar offenders or street offenders. As long as society sees the need to incarcerate lower-class offenders for their misdeeds, it can be argued that society has a duty to punish white-collar offenders who violate the law and that imprisonment is the most appropriate sanction for certain types of white-collar offenders. In addition to providing for fair treatment of offenders, incarceration of white-collar offenders fulfills three other purposes: deterrence, restoration of trust, and public satisfaction (Wilson, 1998).

Regarding deterrence, the incarceration of white-collar offenders keeps those who are incarcerated from committing offenses while they are incarcerated. There is little evidence that incarceration keeps other white-collar employees from committing offenses, although judges and some legal experts tend to believe that incarceration has a potential general deterrent value. After Michael Milken was given his ten-year prison sentence, Columbia law professor Harvey Goldschmid remarked, "The message being sent is that you've got to play within the rules of the game. White-collar crime will be taken seriously and sentenced in a serious way" (Greenwald, 1990: 82).

Restoration of trust occurs when society demonstrates that those who commit offenses violating public trust (which white-collar offenses do) are sanctioned for their offenses (Fleckenstein & Bowers, 2000). Imagine a case where an investor gains the trust of hundreds of individuals and convinces those individuals to invest in a particular business. If the business succeeds, then all is well. If the business fails, then investor trust is reduced. If the business fails because of fraudulent actions on the part of the investor, societal trust is reduced even further. When white-collar offenders are punished, a step is taken toward restoring this violation of trust. Without the appropriate sanction, trust would be reduced dramatically.

Public satisfaction also occurs when white-collar offenders are punished. The traditional thought was that members of the public were ambivalent about the way convicted white-collar criminals should be handled. Research by Cullen et al. (1985) shows that the public recommends sanctions equal to those meted out to street offenders. In short, members of society want white-collar offenders to be punished. It is entirely conceivable that some members of society will take the law into their own hands if they think the justice system has failed in its duty to punish offenders.

Myth #7–White-collar criminals who go to jail or prison experience too easy of a confinement. Not only do members of society want white-collar offenders to be punished, they also want them to "feel the pain" from their punishment. After one business was defrauded, the attorney for the defrauded business said of the offender "[he] is expected to do time, not at a country club federal prison where he can sharpen his tennis game, but at a medium high level security prison where he will live within a real criminal population" (Arndorfer, 1995: 2). This comment is shallow for two reasons. First, it assumes that those in minimum security prisons, including many white-collar criminals, are not "real criminals" when in fact they are as "real as they come." Second, it assumes that the incarceration experience in minimum security prisons is not a punitive experience for white-collar offenders. Many white-collar offenders who have been incarcerated, regardless of the type of institution, are quick to describe their experience as punitive. Here are a few comments made by incarcerated white-collar offenders to journalists that illustrate this point:

- Any time your freedom and liberty are restricted, you're being punished. There is no question. It's confinement, incarceration, call it what you want. It's not what everyone else has.
- People have to realize that we are in prison. We are being punished. I would never do a crime again.
- There are no good prisons just like there are no good funeral homes (Andresky, 1984: 115; *Baltimore Sun*, 1999: A1; Roig-Franzia, 2000: A1).

Prison is a greater lifestyle change for white-collar criminals than for other criminals (Benson & Cullen, 1988). Recall that conventional offenders are more likely to have been previously incarcerated than white-collar offenders are. For most white-collar offenders, prison is a "unique experience" (Breed, 1979: 26). Those who have had a great deal of exposure to prison have been found to prefer prison sentences over alternative sanctions such as intensive probation (Crouch, 1993). Without this previous exposure, white-collar offenders are seen as having a greater sensitivity to incarceration. An incarcerated white-collar offender explained, "You're dropped into the middle of a society whose rules and customs you don't understand" (Mize, 2001 n.p.). Because of their lack of incarceration experience, many white-collar offenders "reject the inmate culture" (Benson & Cullen, 1988: 212). As an example, one white-collar offender told Breed (1979: 52), "I couldn't even adjust to the language. Everybody swore. It was vile and filthy. I was horrified by the whole experience."

Criminologists have considered the way that lower-class youth are judged according to middle-class values when they enter the school system. Referred to as the *middle class measuring rod* by Albert Cohen (1955), the belief is that lower-class children have the odds stacked against them as far as scholastic achievement is concerned because they have learned to live according to a different set of values than those that are used as a barometer for academic success. Differences between lower- and upper-class values are provided in Table 1.2. Based on these subcultural differences, it is possible that an inversion of the middle-class measuring rod occurs when middle– and upper-class offenders enter prison. More specifically, rather than being judged by a middle-class value system, offenders in jails and prisons are likely judged by a *lower-class measuring rod*. What happens is middle- and upper-class offenders become isolated from most offenders and experience incarceration differently than lower-class offenders would. This is not to say that they won't adjust to prison; rather research shows that like lower-class offenders, upper-class offenders eventually adjust to prison life–they simply adjust in different ways (Benson & Cullen, 1988). Their actual experiences and adjustment process are considered in more detail in a later chapter.

TABLE 1.2
DIFFERENCES BETWEEN SOCIALIZATION PATTERNS OF MIDDLE
CLASS AND LOWER CLASS YOUTH

Cultural Trait	Middle Class	Lower Class
Drive, ambition	+	−
Individual responsibility	+	−
Success in classroom	+	−
Deferred gratification	+	−
Long-range planning	+	−
Cultivation of etiquette	+	−
Nonviolence	+	−
Wholesome leisure activity	+	−
Respect for property	+	−

Source: Adapted from Martin et al., 1990.

Myth #8–White-collar criminals never go to prison. Many individuals believe that white-collar criminals never go to prison. Some contend that powerful offenders are protected in a biased justice system. In addition, the fact that victims are sometimes unwilling to cooperate with justice officials means that some offenders escape prison sentences by escaping prosecution. On a related line, many white-collar crime victims simply want their money back and realize that they will not get their money back as quickly, if at all, if the offender is incarcerated (Associated Press, 2001a). Despite these beliefs about the use of prison and jail sanctions to punish offenders, recent evidence shows two interesting trends: 1) more white-collar offenders are being sent to prison and 2) certain factors have been shown to influence the likelihood of incarceration of white-collar offenders.

INCREASES IN THE NUMBER OF WHITE-COLLAR INMATES

In 1970, only eight percent of cases prosecuted by the federal government were white-collar crime cases. By the 1980s, nearly one in four federal criminal prosecutions were white-collar crime prosecutions, and research showed that white-collar offenders' likelihood of going to prison increased between the 1970s and 1980s (Hagan & Palloni, 1986; Maakestad, 1991). Today, one of two white-collar offenders convicted at the federal level will be incarcerated (Higgins,

1999). Estimates from the 1980s suggest that anywhere from ten to 40 percent of the residents in federal minimum security prisons were white-collar offenders (Andresky, 1984). With this increase in the number of white-collar offenders being sent to jail or prison, white-collar offenders represent a significant proportion of federal inmates.

Though not to the same degree, the number of white-collar offenders prosecuted and sentenced to jail or prison in various states has also increased. For instance, of 41,000 fraud cases in U.S. state courts in 1996, 38 percent of the offenders received a jail or prison sentence (Insurance Fraud Bureau of Massachusetts, 2000). A study by the Insurance Fraud Bureau of Massachusetts (2000) of 476 cases of insurance fraud referred to the criminal justice system found the following:

- About 87 percent of the offenders were found guilty and 99 percent of those found guilty received criminal penalties.
- Approximately 44 percent were given jail sentences, and 33 percent were ordered to serve the sentence.
- Sixty percent were given probation or restitution.
- Seventy percent received multiple sentences.

In addition to increases in the number of white-collar offenders being sentenced to prison, there is also evidence that the average prison length for some white-collar offenders has increased. As an illustration, the average prison sentence of criminal cases referred from the Securities Exchange Commission (SEC) to the U.S. Attorney's Office increased from ten months in 1992 to 49 months in 1998 (Reason, 2000). When all federal prison sentences are considered, average sentence lengths increased from 39 months in 1986 to 54 months in 1997 (*The Economist*, 2001).

Indeed, a considerable number of white-collar offenders are receiving prison sentences at the state and federal levels. Two interesting developments have occurred in the occupational arena as a result of these increases. First, because there are now so many white-collar offenders being sent to jail or prison, former white-collar offenders who spent time incarcerated are presently making a living consulting future white-collar inmates about what to expect in their prison stay. Reportedly, David Novak, who spent time in federal prison for insurance fraud, makes over a $100,000 a year sharing his experiences with future white-collar inmates (Garland, 2000). Second, in response to the threat of white-collar employees being sent to jail or prison, some companies have developed policies to follow in case one of their executives receives a jail or prison sentence. These policies focus on maintaining effective public relations so that irrational decisions are not made under pressure. The policies focus on efficient fact gathering and the development of strategies to divert attention away from the company in which the offender was employed (Taylor, 1990).

FACTORS INFLUENCING THE LIKELIHOOD OF INCARCERATION

When white-collar offenses are compared with one another (as opposed to comparing them to street offenses), recent research has shown that three factors play a role in determining whether the offender is incarcerated for his or her misdeeds: harm, blameworthiness, and location (Galvin, 2000; Higgins, 1999; Weisburd et al., 1991). Harm is concerned with the actual losses experienced by victims. More harm means a longer sentence. Judges may even go above sentencing guidelines if harm is quite demonstrable. For instance, one offender who was convicted of swindling investors in the amount of $700 million was given a 30-year prison sentence, which represented a ten-year departure from the maximum sentence recommended in the sentencing guidelines (Galvin, 2000).

Blameworthiness refers to the degree to which the offender can actually be blamed for the offenses (Weisburd et al., 1991). In many white-collar offenses, crime occurs not because of the individual, but because of the expectations placed on individuals in those positions. Basically, employees could leave their jobs, but crime may still be found in those same positions. The practice in the early 1990s of a large retail store paying its automotive repair salespersons by commission is an illustration. Many salespeople went out of their way to add on services so they could make more money. The court ruled that these actions were wrong, although they occurred because of expectations the organization placed on its employees. The retail store was forced to quit paying its automotive salespeople by commission.

Another factor that seems to influence whether a white-collar offender goes to prison is a factor that also determines property value–location, location, location. In particular, recent research cited by Higgins (1999) suggests that whether a white-collar defendant ends up in prison depends on where the case is heard. Transaction Records Access Clearinghouse, a group composed of researchers affiliated with Syracuse University, analyzed data supplied by the Department of Justice. Among other things, the researchers found:

- One in two white-collar offenders convicted in federal court was sent to prison.
- In the western district of Wisconsin, eight of ten white-collar crime convictions resulted in a prison sentence.
- In a district of New Jersey, three of ten white-collar crime convictions resulted in a prison sentence.

Attorneys point out that the role of location may not be as important as is demonstrated by these findings. Certain districts might use different practices to target white-collar offenses. A sting operation in one district could result in an increase in convictions making it seem that the district is more punitive than other districts when in fact actual punitiveness is the same. Or, rural districts may hear less serious cases decreasing the likelihood of prison. Others point out that the definition of white-collar crime used by the Syracuse researchers is not clear, and statistics could be manipulated to show just about anything (Apgar, 1999). Regardless of whether there is disparity between districts, one must ask why there has been an overall increase in the number of white-collar offenders sentenced to jail or prison.

WHY THE INCREASE IN WHITE-COLLAR INMATES?

Thus far, attention has been paid to specific myths about white-collar crime and the increase in the number of white-collar offenders in prisons and jails. To fully understand the plight of incarcerated white-collar offenders, attention must be given to potential reasons why more white-collar offenders are being sent to jail and prison.

Four possible reasons why this increase has occurred include the following:

1. Increases in the number of white-collar offenses committed have led to more prison and jail sentences.
2. More aggressive investigations and prosecutions have made it easier to gather the evidence needed to demonstrate harm and blameworthiness, thus increasing the likelihood of incarceration.
3. A growing public intolerance toward white-collar offenses has made politicians and judges more punitive toward white-collar offenders.
4. Changes in sentencing policies have limited judicial discretion and required stiffer sentences for white-collar offenders.

One possible reason for the increase in the number of white-collar inmates is that there are more white-collar offenses being committed (Janhevich, 1998; Solomon, 1998; Touby, 1994). With technological advances and broader political changes, some have argued that crimes such as computer crime, medical fraud, credit card fraud, and telemarketing fraud have been on the rise (Friedman, 1998; Jesilow et al., 1993; Johnston, 2002). If more offenses are occurring, one would expect more arrests, prosecutions, and convictions of white-collar offenders. Indeed, arrests for fraud and embezzlement went up 25 percent and 56 percent respectively between 1983 and 1992 (Touby, 1994).

Another possible reason for the increase in the number of white-collar inmates is that different agencies have increased their investigation and prosecution efforts (Abelson & Balco, 1992; Schroeder & Barrett, 1996). To increase certain types of white-collar crime investigation in the late 1980s and early 1990s, President George H. Bush announced that an extra $50 million would be provided to investigatory agencies so that the number of officials investigating fraud would double. Around the same time, sophisticated investigative tools typically reserved for street crimes (e.g., search warrants, electronic surveillance, forfeiture proceedings, and undercover investigations) were increasingly used against white-collar offenders (Allen, 1989). The result has been that, in recent times, some types of white-collar offenses have higher clearance rates than many street crimes (see Figure 1.1). For instance, data from Canada suggests that credit card fraud is four times more likely to be cleared than breaking and entering is (Janhevich, 1998). Today, white-collar crime has been cited as the FBI's "largest criminal investigation program, with more than 2,600 pending cases" (Serwer, 2000: 56).

Because more cases were being investigated, prosecutors also

FIGURE 1.1. CLEARANCE RATES FOR OFFENSES IN CANADA*

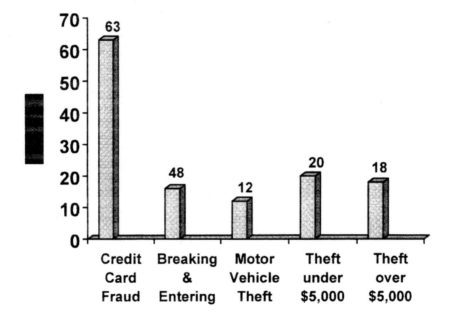

Source: Adapted from Janhevich, 1998.
*Clearance rate refers to the percentage of cases solved by police.

increased their efforts in combating white-collar crime. Criminal prosecutors became better trained on how to aggressively prosecute offenders, and special prosecutor's offices were created to battle certain kinds of white-collar offenses in various jurisdictions across the United States and Canada (Ress, 2001; Quevedo, 1992). In addition, in many states and at the federal level, the discretion typically afforded to judges in white-collar crime cases was taken away from judges, who are often viewed as lenient toward white-collar offenders, and given to prosecutors, who are seen as more punitive (Higgins, 1999).

Changes in sentencing policies also potentially played a role in increasing the number of incarcerated white-collar offenders (Brostoff, 1994; Lott, 1990). Many states increased their penalties for different white-collar offenses. At the federal level, the U.S. Sentencing Commission's Sentencing Guidelines, developed in 1987, controlled judicial discretion by providing a "cookbook" for determining sanctions given to white-collar offenders (O'Toole, 1996; Thompson, 1991). These guidelines made "jail more likely for white-collar offenders" (Reason, 2000: 111) and "sharply increased sentences for white-collar crimes" (Dolinko, 2000: 573).

Another potential reason that more white-collar offenders began to be sentenced to jail or prison is that the public grew increasingly less tolerant of these offenses in the 1980s. A strong victim's rights movement called for tougher responses toward white-collar offenders (Friedrichs, 1996; Morvillo, 1999). Many prosecutors, judges, and political officials likely wanted to display that they too had a strong disdain for these sorts of misdeeds. Many judges and prosecutors, like politicians, want members of the public to see them as "hard on crime." Accordingly, it is plausible that sentences increased to satisfy the public's desire for retribution (Abelson & Balco, 1992; Apgar, 1999; Lore, 1992).

WHITE-COLLAR TIME: THE PRISON EXPERIENCE

Because more white-collar offenders are being incarcerated, it seems necessary that attention be given to how these offenders experience incarceration and what effective strategies can be used to supervise these inmates. The limited amount of research into this area implies that two characteristics of white-collar criminals potentially make them "specially sensitive" to imprisonment: their class background and their lack of experience with the justice system (Benson & Cullen, 1988). Some have argued that this special sensitivity makes incarceration more painful for white-collar offenders than for other offenders (see Breed, 1979; Mann et al., 1980).

To demonstrate the belief that incarceration affects white-collar offenders differently than it affects street criminals, consider the following description of the white-collar inmate experience offered by Breed (1979: 26):

> Prison interferes with the life of any man or woman, but what is interest-
> ing when considering white-collar offenders is, firstly, that they are a
> minority, and secondly, it seems obvious prison affects his way of life
> more than any other section of the prison population. They have more to
> lose. They often have neighbors who themselves never thought they
> would live next to somebody who was actually in prison. They have jobs
> which often entail trust and confidence, and prison means they will lose
> those jobs. They have mortgages, they have cars (often leased), and some-
> times even school [loans], commitments which still have to be met.

Interestingly, though claims have been made that prison is such a
horrible experience for white-collar offenders, other research suggests that white-collar offenders are able to overcome their "special
sensitivity" and adapt to incarceration in meaningful ways (Benson
& Cullen, 1988). The experiences of several offenders who actually
seemed to appreciate what they learned from their incarceration
experience are addressed throughout this book.

SUMMARY AND PLAN OF PRESENTATION

Although more and more white-collar offenders are being incarcerated, our understanding about the way white-collar offenders
experience incarceration has not increased. This book represents
one of the first attempts to address the way that white-collar offenders experience incarceration with an aim toward providing guidance
on effective ways to supervise, manage, and treat white-collar
inmates.

In Chapter 2, the causes of white-collar crime are considered.
Many traditional crime theories are considered in light of their
application to white-collar offenses. These theories are useful in
understanding the behavior of white-collar offenders once it is recognized that they apply somewhat differently to white-collar offenders than they apply to conventional offenders. Understanding the
causes of white-collar crime will aid in helping to prevent offenses in
the future.

Chapter 3 provides a detailed analysis of the kinds of denials
offered by white-collar offenders and the consequences of these
offenses. Attention is given to the kinds of losses suffered by the victim, the victim's family, the offender's family, and society in general.
Understanding the consequences will give criminal justice profes-

sionals the arsenal needed to better understand the past behavior of white-collar offenders.

In Chapter 4, the way white-collar offenders experience prison is discussed. A typology focusing on issues that are specific to white-collar offenders serves as the framework for this chapter. Shedding light on the way white-collar inmates experience incarceration will aid in the general management and supervision of these offenders. In short, if correctional professionals know what white-collar inmates are experiencing, they are in a better position to perform their duties efficiently and effectively.

Chapter 5 considers why white-collar offenders are punished and addresses different community-based sanctions imposed on white-collar offenders. Restorative justice ideals are incorporated to show that the system can help the victim recover from the offense, and hold the offender accountable for his or her offenses. The chapter concludes with a number of tips for correctional officials supervising and treating white-collar offenders. In the final chapter, general recommendations for policy and research are included.

Naturally, some will ask why it is important to understand the incarceration experiences of offenders who have done so much damage to society. There are three related reasons why this is an important area to understand. First, the number of white-collar offenders has increased, but our understanding of their incarceration experiences has not increased. Given that incarceration is an opportunity to prevent future offenses, understanding the most effective ways to handle white-collar offenders so that they choose to avoid crime in the future is a laudable goal.

Second, understanding how white-collar criminals experience incarceration and what methods are appropriate to supervise them helps to understand the experiences of all offenders. Through comparing different types of offenders, understanding about appropriate strategies for all types of offenders will be forthcoming. In short, learning about one type of offender is useful in increasing understanding about all types of offenders.

Third, some might say that it is humane to try to understand the incarceration experiences of offenders. As every correctional professional knows, in a just society, removal from society is the punishment, not the actual specific events occurring in prison. Or, offenders are not put in jail or prison to be punished; rather, they are sent there as their punishment. Anything that can be done to help them cope with their incarceration will make their supervision that much easier.

The intent of this book is not to suggest special or preferential treatment of white-collar offenders; rather, the aim is to suggest that differences between white-collar criminals and street criminals require that slightly different strategies be used to supervise white-collar offenders in jails and prisons.

As an analogy, consider the following story. When this author's daughter Chloe was born last year, on a handful of different occasions people asked me what my son's name was. After all, all babies look alike to many people. When these slightly embarrassing social faux pas occurred, the author politely indicated that her name was Chloe. These individuals looked at a baby and automatically decided its gender. In a similar vein, oftentimes individuals look at offenders and assume that they are all alike. But, they are not alike. There are important differences between different types of offenders that will play a significant role in determining the most effective way to supervise, manage, and treat different kinds of inmates. Although mistaking a baby's gender does not have significant consequences, ignoring differences between offenders' can have important consequences.

APPLIED CRITICAL THINKING: WHAT DO YOU THINK?

1. Is white-collar crime a serious problem in our society?
2. Why should white-collar criminals be incarcerated?
3. How are white-collar criminals different from street criminals?
4. What characteristics of white-collar criminals might influence their incarceration experience?
5. Why are more white-collar offenders being incarcerated?
6. Should white-collar offenders be separated from other offenders?
7. Why is it important to understand the experiences of white-collar inmates?

Chapter 2

MOTIVATIONS FOR WHITE-COLLAR CRIME

INTRODUCTION

Theorists have sought to understand the causes of human behavior since civilization was founded. Part of the rationale for this focus on causality involves the belief that through understanding causes, appropriate intervention and prevention methods can be implemented and followed. The search for causality extends to criminologists' efforts to explain white-collar crime. The following examples from real cases occurring over the last couple of years illustrate this point:

- Real estate salesman Krishan Chari was sentenced to eight years in prison after he used his position to steal millions from the Sterling Title Agency. As a result of his fraud, the company president was forced to lay off 45 employees and file for bankruptcy (Modic, 2001).
- An attorney involved in orchestrating the business side of a telemarketing fraud ring was sentenced to nine years in prison. The attorney denied his role in the fraudulent activity and claimed that he "simply offered legal services to what he believed were legitimate companies" (Rivera, 1998: n.p.).
- One white-collar offender justified her actions on the grounds that she stole $246,000 from her employer because she "self-medicated" herself with shopping sprees to battle her depression. The judge believed her defense and sentenced her leniently (*News Gazette Champaign*, 2001).
- A woman who was embarrassed to admit to her husband that

she overspent and didn't have the money for their son's tuition stole from her company to fix her financial bind. She ended up embezzling $511,455 (Hansen, 2000).

Each of these case descriptions provides a hint of explanation. In the first case, the real estate attorney was able to steal because he had the opportunity to do so. In the second illustration, the attorney denied that his conduct was intentionally criminal. In the third scenario, the shopaholic's actions were explained as a disease. In the final case, the woman stole to cover her son's tuition because she got herself into a financial bind. These four explanations are among the common explanations offered for white-collar crime. Just as important is the fact that understanding causality has direct implications for corrections professionals. Because more and more white-collar offenders are being placed under some form of correctional supervision, in attempting to fix the problem so that the offender will not commit future offenses on release from correctional supervision, it is imperative that the underlying motivations for the behavior are accurately understood.

Consider the following anecdote. While working on this particular chapter, the author developed some severe back pains. Trying to figure out why his back hurt so much, the author eventually attributed the pain to a new chair he was using in one of his classrooms. Because the pain started around the same time he started using the chair, the connection was obvious. So was the fix—don't sit in the new chair. After avoiding the chair for a few days, the pain continued to surface at different times. Incidentally, while the author was experiencing his unexplained back pains, his daughter was experiencing teething pains. On many nights, the eight-month-old would wake up in the middle of the night only to be consoled when she was placed in bed with the author and his wife.

One such night when the daughter needed consolation from her teething pain, the author was awoken at four in the morning with the worst back pains yet. On waking up, he realized that his daughter was kicking him with her left leg straight into his lower back. Finally, the source of the pain was identified. The fix? Thereafter when the author's daughter needed consolation from her teething pains, his wife agreed to sleep in the side of the bed targeted by the baby's kicking. Because the author's wife is far smaller than he is, she could lay further away from the "baby kicking danger zone" and still be on the bed.

The point of this story is simple. If the wrong explanation is identified, then the problem will continue. If the correct explanation is identified, then appropriate intervention methods can be developed. Of course, unlike pinpointing the source of the author's back pain, figuring out the cause of white-collar crime is no easy task. As white-collar crime expert Jay Albanese (1999: 17) tells us, it is likely "that no single factor 'causes' [white-collar crime] or any other crime." Indeed, what motivates one person to commit a crime in the workplace may be different that what motivates another person to commit the same offense (just as the cause of backaches may vary from person to person).

This chapter addresses several motivations for white-collar crime. In addressing these motivations, a microlevel approach focusing on explaining individuals' actions is taken. Given that this text is focusing on the incarceration experience of white-collar offenders, and ways to effectively manage offenders, it seems more useful to focus on explanations focusing on the "behavior of individuals" as opposed to the "behavior of law," the latter of which is concerned with the way that broader social and political structures influence law development, enforcement, and the interrelationships between the legal structure and other societal institutions (Green, 1997). By way of introduction into causality in general, the explanations for white-collar crime to be addressed in this chapter begin with a broader theory (routine activities theory) and then turn to the specific motivations for white-collar offenses.

ROUTINE ACTIVITIES AND WHITE-COLLAR CRIME

Routine activity theory was developed by Cohen and Felson (1979) in the late 1970s. The theory posits that crime occurs when three elements are present: 1) a suitable target, 2) the absence of a capable guardian, and 3) a motivated offender. Among other things, the original conception of the theory focused on the way that broader societal changes in the 1960s contributed to crime (e.g., fewer people staying home made for fewer capable guardians to prevent crime in an era when more goods or suitable targets were available for a growing number of motivated offenders, see Payne and Gainey, 2001). In other words, as society changes, the nature of crime will also change (Felson, 1998; Nicholson et al., 2000).

This premise certainly relates to white-collar crime. With changes in various ways that companies "do business" based on technological advances, new opportunities for white-collar offenses have surfaced over the past two decades, and opportunity is seen as a central element needed for white-collar crime (Weisburd et al., 1990). For example, computer criminals would never have had the opportunity to commit computer crimes if computers were never even invented. Moreover, the kinds of computer crimes have changed in society as computer usage increased. With increases in Internet usage, there have been increases in Internet fraud. The National White Collar Crime Center cites auction fraud (64% of complaints), non-delivery of items (22% of complaints), and credit card frauds (5% of complaints) as the top three Internet frauds in the mid-1990s (Bonnvissuto, 2001). Just a few years before, credit card frauds topped the list. With increases in Internet auctions and businesses, the kinds of Internet crimes shifted. This is consistent with a structural application of routine activities theory.

Routine activities theory can also apply at the individual level when the three specific elements of the theory are considered. An individual-level application yields a better understanding of individual motivations for white-collar crime and provides a framework from which a consideration of the numerous motivations for white-collar crime can be addressed. First, regarding the absence of a capable guardian, white-collar crimes will be more likely to occur when there is nothing to stop potential offenders from committing their misdeeds. As an illustration, Nadler (2000: 16) pointed out that many white-collar crimes occur "because the institutional structure [white-collar offenders] faced was so riddled with loopholes." Others suggest that the lack of enforcement threats also limit the ability of institutions to guard against victimization (Krueger, 1999; Sayre, 1998). However, according to routine activities theory, the lack of a capable guardian is not enough for a crime to occur; rather the other elements must also be present.

For instance, there must also be a suitable target—something that the white-collar criminal wants. These targets can either be the business itself or the consumer. When consumers are targeted, it is believed that older consumers with a sizable income or savings make up the bulk of targets, not because older persons are vulnerable, but because of the trusting relationship that offenders develop with the victims (Ganzini et al., 1990; Locy, 1998). The kinds of targets focused on by white-collar offenders has prompted Ganzini and his colleagues (1990: 61) to quip, "the term 'white-collar' not only describes the deceivers but the deceived."

Note that to reduce the possibility of capable guardians preventing the offenders from seizing the property of the victim, the offender usually finds a way to get the "suitable target" to trust the offender. Here are a few examples of this process:

- One fraudulent investor was so bold that he printed the words "In God We Trust" on his business cards that were distributed to his potential victims–most of whom incidentally were elderly. Eventually he scammed 6.2 million dollars from 127 victims (Reed, 2000).

- A fraudulent stock broker stole $390,000 from an 88-year-old woman with Alzheimer's. The offender knew the woman since he was a child (Brewer, 1999).

- A victim whose family lost $560,000 through a fraudulent investment scheme saw their offender as a trustworthy individual. She commented, "He posed as a religious guy. We would hold hands and pray around the dinner table. We trusted him." (Ruth, 2000: 1C).

- One prosecutor described how a white-collar criminal chose his suitable targets: "He would get coaches from his kids' soccer teams, people they knew personally. He'd screw a friend of the family" (Nowlin, 2001: n.p.).

- Using the trust afforded to him from his employer, an employee of a large corporation recently accessed a list of social security numbers for the corporations' employees, "and then one by one [used] the employees' identities for fraudulent purposes" (Davis & Burt, 2001: 89).

Although suitable targets and the absence of capable guardians must be present for a white-collar crime to occur, these elements are not enough to explain crime from a routine activities perspective. Instead, the third element, the presence of a motivated offender, must be present. In fact, it seems safe to suggest that this is the most important element of the theory's assumptions—if no motivated offender is present, then a crime, whether a white-collar crime or some other crime, simply will not occur. As stated in the introduction of this chapter, the motivations for offending are particularly relevant for corrections professionals in that once the motivations are identified, intervention methods can be established.

Cohen and Felson (1979) never directly considered what the term "*motivated offender*" means in regards to white-collar crime. Using the white-collar crime literature and several prominent criminological theories, however, a number of possible motivations become apparent and are addressed in the following section. The motivations to be considered include the following:

- Pleasure seeking
- Learned behavior
- Weak bonds with society
- Low self-control
- Personality flaws
- Stress/Strain
- Greed
- Gambling
- Drugs
- Denials

Keep in mind that motivations will vary from offense to offense and offender to offender, and that these are only plausible explanations of behavior. There is no universally accepted explanation for white-collar crime, but the possible motivations offer a guide from which intervention practices can evolve. Indeed, for each possible motivation, a specific problem may coincide with the motivation. These problems have implications for corrections professionals who are interested in reducing the possibility that the offender reoffends. The relationship between motivations, problems, and implications for corrections is outlined in Table 2.1.

TABLE 2.1
WHITE-COLLAR CRIME MOTIVATIONS, PROBLEMS, AND IMPLICATIONS FOR CORRECTIONS EMPLOYEES

Motivation	Problem	Implication for Corrections
Pleasure seeking	Pleasure seeking in its purest form (with no regard for pain or negative consequences) is actually an irrational activity that can harm the individual and associates.	Teach individual that there can be negative consequences from the pursuit of pleasure.
Learned behavior	Individuals may learn from others the techniques and reasons for committing white-collar offenses.	If individuals can learn inappropriate behavior and values, through appropriate guidance from corrections professionals, they can also learn values consistent with law abiding behavior.
Weak bonds with society	Individuals who are not attached to society or do not believe in societal rules are prone to law violations.	Attachments can be strengthened by involving individuals in different institutions and increasing the stake individuals have in conformity.
Low self-control	Some people are not able to resist temptations because they can't control themselves.	Self-control level can be changed through an effective turning point such as training or rehabilitation.
Personality flaws	Certain personalities are more prone towards white-collar crime.	By recognizing one's tendencies towards misbehavior, one can make changes.
Stress/Strain	A culture of competition and emphasis on success, combined with obstacles to success, creates stress which leads some to commit white-collar crimes.	Individuals need to learn other ways to define success.
Greed	Inherent desire to want more even when needs are met leads to white-collar crimes	Individuals need to reevaluate priorities to consider the source of their greed.
Gambling	Addiction to taking monetary risks in the form of gambling leads to misdeeds.	Individuals need to overcome their addiction just as they would overcome a drug addiction.
Drugs	Substance abuse causes white-collar crime through either impaired judgement or need to pay for drug habit.	Substance abusers need to overcome their addiction and deal with the problems that caused the addiction in the first place.
Denials	White-collar criminals rationalize their behavior as appropriate by offering any number of denials, excuses, or justifications.	Individuals need to understand that they are responsible for their behavior and that there are consequences from their actions.

PLEASURE SEEKING

A classic belief about the cause of crime is that individuals are rational beings who will weigh the pleasure they will get from a particular course of action against the possible pain they would receive from that course of action. If the pleasure outweighs the pain, then that particular course of action becomes likely. Traced to Cesare Beccaria's (1764) *On Crimes and Punishments* and referred to as deterrence theory or rational choice theory, this perspective has been used to explain the behavior of white-collar criminals, and in fact, because of the rational nature of white-collar offenders, "would appear to be especially applicable to white-collar offenders" (Friedrichs, 1996: 226). Said one author team writing about white-collar crime, "If a criminally motivated person believes that the opportunity to profit is greater than the potential risk associated with discovery, it is crime time" (Turner & Stephenson, 1993: 57).

As far as the pleasure versus pain principle, the famous 1970s cop show "*Baretta*" starring Robert Blake summed up deterrence ideals in the show's opening theme song that included the lyrics, "Don't do the crime if you can't do time." This line of reasoning is traced to Beccaria who contended that in order for punishment to outweigh pleasure, the punishment must meet three criteria: 1) it must be certain, 2) it must slightly outweigh the pleasure one would get from committing the act, and 3) it must be swift. In regard to white-collar crime, critics note that none of these criteria are fulfilled insofar as the criminal justice system's response to white-collar crime is concerned. They argue: 1) there is no certainty of punishment; 2) the punishment given to white-collar offenders is too lenient, and 3) due to court delays, continuances, and appeals, the punishment of white-collar offenders is rarely swift (Conley, 2000; Eitle, 2000; Posner, 1980). Consequently, it is believed that white-collar crime occurs because of the inherent seeking of pleasure in the face of only a minimal (if not nonexistent) threat of punishment (Wells, 1990).

On the other hand, the fact that white-collar crime is seen as a rational activity committed by rational beings leads some to suggest that white-collar crime can be deterred if certain conditions are present (Friedrichs, 1996; Higgins, 1999; Pontell et al., 1984; Weisburd & Waring, 2001). In considering deterrence and white-collar crime, criminologists discuss two types of deterrence: specific deterrence and general deterrence. Specific deterrence ideals suggest that a specific white-collar offender's actions can be deterred in the future if he or she is punished in an appropriate fashion. General deterrence ideals suggest that the actions of the general white-collar population are deterred when they hear that other white-collar offenders are being punished.

Research shows that many judges base their sanctions on the belief that punishment will keep others from committing offenses. Wheeler and his colleagues (1988a: 13), for instance, quote a judge who said, "My primary concern in the typical white-collar crime case is general deterrence—getting a message out to people in the business community who might be tempted to do the same thing." It is common, however, to hear individuals complain that prisons and jails are too lavish and cannot keep individuals from offending. When the author hears students make these claims, he always asks them if they would rather live where they currently live or in prison. Not one student has ever responded that they wish they were institutionalized. So, general deterrence, though very difficult to measure, likely occurs to a degree. In fact, stiff penalties for many white-collar offenders are based on ideals of general deterrence (Boss and George, 1992).

Although prison and jail may serve as a general deterrent for some, research on the imprisonment of white-collar offenders shows that "a prison sentence does not have a specific deterrent effect" (Weisburd & Waring, 2001: 113). In fact, in direct opposition of deterrence, some argue that punishment that is too severe may actually cause an offender to reoffend rather than keep the offender from reoffending. Weisburd and Waring's research did not find that punishment contributes to future white-collar offenses, but the possibility nonetheless exists. Known as the brutalization argument, it is well accepted that punishments that offenders see as too severe may have the opposite effect of deterrence in that future misbehavior may increase rather than decrease.

This is certainly a possibility as far as the punishment of white-collar offenders is concerned. Because so many white-collar offenders deny their criminality or feel unjustly punished, it is feasible that some white-collar criminals who feel unjustly punished will become more hardened rather than rehabilitated. To avoid this, corrections professionals may need to employ strategies during the treatment phase of correctional supervision to help offenders see that they indeed committed criminal acts that warranted a response from the justice process and also to help them see that the unguided pursuit of pleasure can result in pain for the offender, his or her family, and his or her associates. However, some contend that in many places the purpose of incarcerating white-collar offenders is simply incapacitation (e.g., separation from society) rather than rehabilitation, and this may explain why studies show that half of incarcerated white-collar offenders reoffend after their release from prison or jail (Weisburd et al., 1993).

Deterrence theory is criticized on a number of grounds including suggestions that the theory 1) oversimplifies decision making, 2) does not adequately explain why rational individuals still choose to commit crime, and 3) exaggerates the actual deterrent effect of punishment. Perhaps one of the most useful criticisms of deterrence theory is offered by Coleman (1992: 6) who pointed out that "a theory of deterrence must be combined with some notion of what motivates people to commit crime in the first place." Essentially, when asked what causes white-collar crime, pure deterrence theory proponents would respond that the pursuit of pleasure with minimal perceived risk of punishment is the source of white-collar crime. Coleman takes it a step further and asks what motivates individuals to seek out pleasure in the first place. Depending on the particular white-collar offense and offender, the answer to Coleman's question can be found in any of the motivations addressed in the remainder of this chapter.

WHITE-COLLAR CRIME AS LEARNED BEHAVIOR

Many criminologists, including Edwin Sutherland, who created the concept of white-collar crime, contend that white-collar crime is learned from others in a learning process similar to the way any type of behavior is learned. Sutherland's theory of criminal learning is referred to as differential association and is set forth in nine principles he first outlined in his *Principles of Criminology* book published in 1939 (see Table 2.2). The general assumption of Sutherland's theory is that criminal behavior is learned through a process of communication with small interpersonal groups, and that criminals learn techniques and reasons for committing crimes from these small interpersonal groups. Those who learn definitions favorable to law violations are more likely to commit crimes than those who do not.

TABLE 2.2
SUTHERLAND'S DIFFERENTIAL ASSOCIATION THEORY

1. Criminal behavior is learned.
2. Criminal behavior is learned in interaction with other persons in a process of communication.
3. The principle part of the learning of criminal behavior occurs within intimate personal groups.
4. Learning criminal behavior includes learning the techniques of committing the crime, which are sometimes very complicated and sometimes very simple, and learning the specific direction of motives, drives, rationalizations, and attitudes.
5. The specific direction of motives and drives is learned from perceptions of various aspects of the legal code as being favorable or unfavorable.
6. A person becomes criminal when he or she perceives more favorable than unfavorable consequences to violating the law.
7. Differential associations may vary in frequency, duration, priority, and intensity.
8. The process of learning criminal behavior by association with criminal and anticriminal patterns involves all of the mechanisms involved in any other learning.
9. Although criminal behavior is an expression of general needs and values, it is not excused by those general needs and values as noncriminal behavior is also an expression of the same needs and values.

Source: Adapted from Sutherland (1939).

Although Sutherland developed his theory to explain all criminal behavior, he took several opportunities to illustrate how his theory explains white-collar crime. Consider the following comments from Sutherland (1983: 246):

> White-collar criminals, like professional thieves, are seldom recruited from juvenile delinquents. As a part of the process of learning practical business, a young man with idealism and thoughtfulness for others is inducted into white-collar crime. In many cases, he is ordered by managers to do things he regards as unethical or illegal, while in other cases he learned from those who have the same rank as his own how they make a success. He learns specific techniques of violating the law, together with definitions of situations in which those techniques may be used.

To illustrate this process, Sutherland often relied on rich qualitative descriptions that provided a detailed overview of specific white-collar criminals "learning the ropes." Here is just one example in which he quoted a shoe salesperson who learned the rationale for selling misfitting shoes from his manager:

> [the manager told the salesperson] My job is to move out shoes and I have you to assist in this. I am perfectly glad to fit a person with a pair of shoes if we have his size, but I am willing to misfit him if it is necessary in order to sell him a pair of shoes. I expect you to do the same. If you do not like this, someone else can have your job. While you are working for me, I expect you to have no scruples how you sell your shoes (Sutherland, 1983: 244).

Research in the 1940s and 1950s both questioned and confirmed the usefulness of differential association theory's ability to explain white-collar crime (Poveda, 1994). Today, it is generally accepted that inadequate or inappropriate training may foster attitudes conducive to crime in the workplace (Keenan et al., 1985; Maddocks, 1992; Payne, 1998; Wright & Cullen, 2000). Coleman (1994: 199) offers one of the more compelling approvals of the theory stating, "Sutherland's contentions that criminal behavior is learned can hardly be challenged, and his forceful insistence on this point has been of lasting benefit to modern criminology."

Sutherland's learning theory has been criticized on a number of grounds including suggestions that the theory (1) is too abstract, (2) is too narrow, (3) does not explain the original source of crime, (4) does not explain how definitions change from favorable to unfavorable and vise versa, and (5) is virtually impossible to test (Coleman, 1994; Martin et al., 1990). Despite these criticisms of this ever-popular learning theory, the underlying assumption of learning theory is critical to corrections professionals: If individuals learn values and techniques conducive to criminal behavior, then those who have learned these values and techniques can also "relearn" values and techniques conducive to law-abiding behavior. Indeed, some have speculated that "white-collar criminals often learn to rethink their attitudes and how they treat people" (Reguly, 1992: 107). Along this line of reasoning, Pratt and Cullen (2000: 953) reminded us that "research on offender rehabilitation reveals that . . . programs that target anti-social attitudes/peers for change achieve among the highest reductions in recidivism." The clear implication is that white-collar offenders can be rehabilitated.

WEAK SOCIETAL BONDS AND WHITE-COLLAR CRIME

Another motivation for white-collar crime lies in the possibility that some offenders may have weak bonds with society. In talking about individuals' bonds to society, criminologists often rely on different versions of a theoretical perspective broadly referred to as control theory. Control theory, unlike the other explanations, asks "why don't people commit crime" as opposed to "why do people commit crime" (Hirschi, 1969). The answer control theorists offer is that most individuals refrain from criminal behavior because they have strong bonds with society.

Travis Hirschi's (1969) control theory, described in *Causes of Delinquency*, is among the most popular control theories considered by criminologists. According to Hirschi, individuals' bonds to society are composed of four elements: attachment, belief, involvement, and commitment. *Attachment* refers to the degree to which individuals are attached to their family, their job, or another conventional institution. *Belief* refers to the degree to which one believes in, and agrees with, the rules of society. *Involvement* is concerned with the degree to which individuals are involved in activities that are accepted by society. *Commitment* refers to the degree to which individuals are committed to meeting the goals and expectations set by society.

In theory, the stronger one's attachment, belief, involvement, and commitment, the more likely one will refrain from crime, and when any of these elements become weak, the less likely one will refrain from misconduct. In essence, as the bond becomes weaker, the likelihood of crime increases. For white-collar criminals, control theorists would argue that at least one of the elements of the bond has become weakened, causing the white-collar offender to transgress.

In one of the few tests of the theory's applicability to white-collar crime, Lasley (1988) surveyed 435 executives of a large multinational automobile company. He found that those executives who were most strongly bonded to their bosses, coworkers, and the company were least likely to commit criminal acts on the job. On the other hand, in terms of organizational offending (e.g., instances where individuals commit crimes against consumers for the organization), it is equally reasonable to suggest an opposite relationship for those white-collar employees who have strong bonds with their organization. Specifically, some note that those who are strongly attached to an organization, its goals, and its expectations will actually be more inclined to violate the law if the managers in the organization expect them to do so (Friedrichs, 1996).

As with the other explanations for white-collar crime, control theory has implications for corrections professionals. If certain offenders have weak bonds with society, or overly strong bonds with their organization, then measures can be taken to increase the white-collar offender's overall bond to society. In other words, it would be prudent to increase the white-collar offender's conformity to societal expectations so that he or she feels that there is too much to lose by reoffending. Employment, stable relationships, and solid but realistic goals are just a few factors that have been found to increase an individual's stake in conformity (Sampson & Laub, 1993).

SELF-CONTROL AND WHITE-COLLAR CRIME

Another explanation for white-collar crime is that offenders have a low self-control and are not able to control their desires for whatever they are seeking. Described by Gottfredson and Hirschi (1990) in their seminal work *A General Theory of Crime*, the theory is based on the belief that all crimes can be explained by one general theory. Thus, they argued that the causes of white-collar crime are no different than the causes of conventional crime. To support this assertion, a few years prior to publishing this work that contained the full version of their theory, Hirschi and Gottfredson (1987) explained how their theory specifically applied to white-collar criminals. Briefly, using a thread of rational choice theory as a foundation, they argued that the motive in all crimes is personal benefit and that both white-collar criminals and conventional criminals commit their crimes because they receive some form of benefit from the violation. Of course, the question that comes up is why all individuals don't commit crime in the pursuit of personal benefit. The answer, according to Gottfredson and Hirschi, is that individuals with a low self-control are those who will take risks to obtain their personal benefits.

Before using the phrase "self-control," Hirschi and Gottfredson (1987: 959) first used the concept of criminality to describe individuals' propensity for criminal behavior and offered the following definition of the concept: "the tendency of individuals to pursue short-term gratification in the most direct way with very little considera-tion for long-term consequences." Later they used the notion of "self-control," which they described as "the individual characteristic relevant to the commission of criminal acts" (Gottfredson and Hirschi, 1990: 88).

Self-control, they contend, comes from the lack of appropriate parenting received during one's childhood. They further suggest that one's self-control is stable throughout one's life and that when confronted with opportunities those with a lower self-control are more likely to commit criminal acts than those with a higher self-control. As far as why self-control affects crime, Gottfredson and Hirschi (1990: 90) argued that those with a low self-control are more likely to be "impulsive, insensitive, physical (as opposed to mental), risk-taking, short-sighted, and non-verbal."

Their theory has been subjected to many tests (Arneklev et al., 1998; Grasmick et al., 1993; Pratt & Cullen, 2000) and a great deal of criticism (Akers, 1991; Geis, 2000; Reed & Yeager, 1996). In terms of white-collar crime, both indirect and direct comments in the white-collar crime literature suggest that some white-collar offenders may indeed possess low self-controls, and when given the opportunity, choose to commit criminal acts on the job. Consider, for instance, the suggestion that many of the frauds arising out of the savings and loan cisis were the result of "taking huge risks" (Will et al., 1998: 368). Others have also described risk taking as an important factor that contributes to white-collar crime (Wheeler, 1992; Wheeler et al., 1988a). In fact, Wheeler et al. (1988b: 331) used the phrase "high-risk ego gratifiers" to describe those white-collar offenders who respond to obstacles in their pursuit of upward mobility in their organization by "bending or breaking the rules."

Of course, risk taking is not the only predictor of white-collar crime, and other indicators of low self-control have also been cut suggested to contribute to white-collar crime. Inadvertently describing his impulsivity and insensitivity, one white-collar offender com-mented, "I wondered if these guys are supposed to be the best at security and I can get past them then, what am I?" (Nash, 1998: 101). This same offender's lawyer said that the offender asked rhetorically "wouldn't this be cool." As further evidence of a possible low self-control among white-collar offenders, Albrecht et al. (1984) de-scribed thirteen motivations of offenders who committed internal fraud in the United States and Canada (see Figure 2.1). Many of these motivations (e.g., living beyond one's means, temptation, desire to lead wild life) are analogous to the characteristics that Gottfredson and Hirschi claim are indicative of a low self-control.

Some point out that Gottfredson and Hirschi's theory cannot adequately explain the behavior of many white-collar offenders because many white-collar offenders had to have a high self-control in order to initially enter their occupation, and many have "stable employ-

FIGURE 2.1 MOTIVATIONS FOR INTERNAL FRAUD

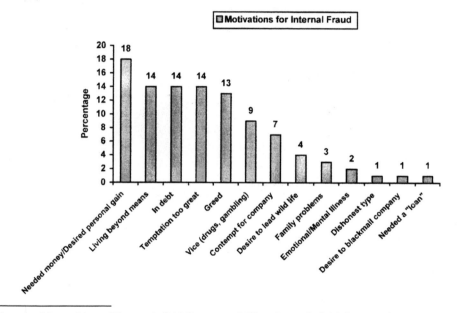

Source: Adapted from Albanese's (1999) review of Albrecht et al's (1984) research on 212 frauds committed in Canada and the U.S.

ment histories" that would be unexpected if they actually had a low level of self-control (Weisburd & Waring, 2001: 55). Benson and Moore (1992) reconciled this by suggesting that different levels of self-control among white-collar offenders relate to the actual motivations for the offenses. They cite three levels and corresponding motivations:

1. Low self-control white-collar offenders commit their offenses because they are impulsive.

2. High self-control offenders commit their offenses to satisfy their egos.
3. In the middle self-control offenders take advantage of opportunities to deal with personal problems that arise.

Other criticisms of Gottfredson and Hirschi's theory are based on the belief that the theory oversimplifies the causal relationship (Geis, 2000). For instance, Reed and Yeager (1996) noted the theory underestimates the role of opportunity, fails to adequately address organizational offending, and ignores the importance of on-the-job socialization. The latter criticism is echoed by Pratt and Cullen (2000) and Akers (1991) who noted that the role of learning self-control cannot be ignored.

The belief that self-control can be learned has direct implications for corrections professionals. Though Gottfredson and Hirschi claim that self-control remains stable throughout one's life, research suggests that major turning points in individual's lives (getting married, getting a job, etc.) can influence self-control levels (Sampson & Laub, 1993). What this means is that the punishment of white-collar offenders can serve as a turning point that alters self-control levels. Theoretically, given the appropriate intervention, white-collaroffenders should be able to develop a level of self-control that will help them to resist the temptation of future misconduct.

PERSONALITIES AND WHITE-COLLAR CRIME

Somewhat related to Gottfredson and Hirschi's claims that a low self-control contributes to crime, some authors believe that white-collar offenders commit their offenses due to certain personality characteristics. In one of the few studies considering personalities and white-collar crime, Collins and Schmidt (1993) surveyed 365 white-collar inmates and 344 non-white-collar offenders. They found that white-collar offenders have "greater tendencies toward irresponsibility, lack of dependability, and disregard of rules and social norms" (p. 295). The major difference between white-collar offenders and nonoffenders, according to the authors, is social conscientiousness.

Collins and Schmidt defined social conscientiousness by breaking the phrase down into its component parts. *Social* captures the study's finding that offenders were more involved in extra-curricular activities, and more prone to social extraversion (having a lot of friends, directing group projects, being effective in social situations). *Conscientiousness* refers to the low disregard for norms and values, and the lack of responsibility and dependability. Taken together, as extraverts, white-collar offenders are believed to get themselves into situations where they have the opportunity to offend, and their lack of conscience provides them the wherewithal to do so.

Many criminologists see personality explanations as less than useful. White-collar crime expert James Coleman (1994) was particularly vocal about the problems he sees with basing white-collar crime explanations on personality factors. He begins by noting that there is very little empirical support for the belief that white-collar criminals have different personalities than the nonoffending group of white-collar employers. Many individuals, he further contends, have "white-collar" personalities that emerge in pursuit of the goals promoted by the U.S. culture of competition. Only some, however, turn to crime. Thus, many individuals are "reckless," "antisocial," and "egocentric." Not all reckless, antisocial, and egocentric individuals turn to white-collar crime. Moreover, he pointed out that explanations based on personality factors ignore structural demands and the influence of the environment (discussed in the next section).

Despite the "thumbs-down" review from Coleman, personality explanations have some utility for corrections professionals. Although personality factors fail to explain all white-collar crimes, it is possible that at least some of the white-collar offenders that corrections professionals supervise committed their offenses, in part, due to some aspect of their personality. The implication from this is that by recognizing which characteristics contribute to the misconduct, actions can be taken so that the offender can limit the influence that those characteristics have on the possibility of reoffending. For instance, if an offender is generally extraverted and has virtually no degree of concern about others, he or she may recognize that this personal extraversion could lead to situations where this lack of concern for others creates problems. By recognizing that this could happen, the offender should be prepared to make decisions that will be in accordance with the law.

STRESS/STRAIN

Another common explanation for white-collar crime is that offenders have experienced some form of economic strain or other type of stress that causes them to commit their offenses (Coleman, 1994; Vaughan, 1983). Strain or stress explanations are traced to Robert Merton's (1938) "Social Structure and Anomie" article in which he described a typology for understanding the way that individuals respond to blocked societal goals. The thrust of Merton's strain theory is founded on the following assumptions:

- Our capitalist society promotes goals of financial success.
- Individuals are expected to follow certain legitimate means to attain those goals.
- Some individuals will have the opportunities to obtain their goals blocked.
- When opportunities are blocked individuals will adapt by accepting or rejecting the goals, legitimate means, or both.

Merton describes five modes of adaptation to describe the ways individuals respond to goals and means of society. *Conformists* are individuals who accept the goals and means proscribed by society and avoid violations of societal norms and laws. *Innovators* are individuals who accept goals of economic success but reject the legitimate means to attain these goals, and find an illegitimate method to achieve financial success. *Ritualists* are those who reject the goals of society but accept the legitimate means prescribed by society. *Retreatists* are individuals who reject both the goals and means prescribed by society and, according to Merton, include those with substance abuse problems and those who have become isolated from society. *Rebels* are those who reject both the goals and the means of society and replace the goals and means with those that would be seen as radical by the majority of society.

Merton developed this theory to describe lower-class offending, and consequently his theory has been criticized on the grounds that it does not explain crimes of the upper class. Messner and Rosenfeld (2001: 55) thought that this criticism "reflects a somewhat oversimplified reading of Merton's arguments." Rosoff and his coauthors (1998: 400) seem to agree, writing, "The standard of material success is not an objective one but exists on a sliding scale—so that even the relatively well-off may feel their aspirations are blocked and may thus resort to crime to achieve culturally defined goals." Indeed, when the underlying assumptions of the theory are considered (e.g., that frustration results when goals are not obtained) it is certainly easy to see how his typology addresses many types of white-collar crime. The relationship between Merton's theory and white-collar offending is outlined in Table 2.3.

As shown in Table 2.3, the vast majority of white-collar employees are law abiding and would be described as conformists in Merton's typology. Innovators would include those white-collar offenders who experience strain as the result of blocked goals, and subse-

TABLE 2.3
MERTON'S MODES OF ADAPTATION AND WHITE-COLLAR CRIME

Mode of Adaptation	Societal Goals	Legitimate Means	Example
Conformity	Accepts	Accepts	White-collar employees who do not violate the law and work hard at meeting the organization's goals.
Innovator	Accepts	Rejects	White-collar employees who bend or break the rules either for direct personal benefit or for the benefit of the organization.
Ritualist	Rejects	Accepts	White-collar employees who do what they are expected but do not work hard toward achieving the goals of the organization.
Retreatist	Rejects	Rejects	White-collar employees who seek an escape from their job or from society by 1) abusing drugs or alcohol, or 2) isolating themselves physically or emotionally.
Rebel	Rejects/Replaces	Rejects/Replaces	White-collar employees who reject and replace the goals of the organization in such a way that the offender is committing the crime against the organization or society in pursuit of nonfinancial goals.

Source: Adapted from Merton (1938).

quently follow illegitimate means to obtain the goals they have set for themselves or their company. Ritualists would include those white-collar employers who do what they are expected, but do not work toward any goals. Retreatists would include those white-collar offenders who commit their offenses due to substance abuse problems (discussed later). Finally, rebels would be white-collar offenders who have rejected society's goals and means and replaced them with their own goals and means. Examples would include what Calavita et al. (1997) referred to as collective embezzlement, or crime by the organization against the organization. Common in the savings and loan crisis, the goal in many collective embezzlement cases is company failure so that governmental insurance programs would pay the organization's profit. Those participating in collective embezzlement reject the standard goal of success, replace it with the goal of failure, and reject the legitimate ways to attain success.

While some claim that Merton's typology does not adequately explain white-collar crime, a point the author rejects, others say that his approach is not really a theory in the classic sense, but a typology. There is a certain degree of validity to this claim. However, to counter this criticism, it is significant to note that Merton's "non-theory" typology contributed to a great deal of theory building, and many of these theories that evolved out of Merton's strain theory say a great deal about the motivations for white-collar misconduct. Four such theories are (1) Vaughan's theory of organizational misconduct, (2) Coleman's culture of competition theory, (3) Messner and Rosenfeld's (2001) *Crime and the American Dream*, and (4) Agnew's strain theory.

Diane Vaughan's (1992) theory of organizational offending uses Merton's typology as a framework to argue that the best way to understand white-collar crime is by linking together an understanding of macrolevel goals and microlevel motivations. Doing this, she argued, helps to understand how the interrelationships between the organization and the individual contribute to crimes committed in the workplace. She described three major elements of her theory:

1. A competitive environment generating pressures for organizational law violations.
2. Organizational characteristics such as structure and processes providing opportunities.

3. A relationship between organizations and regulators in the regulatory environment that minimizes the likelihood of detection and prosecution.

Vaughan stressed that within the competitive environment that faces a low likelihood of detection, individuals choose their actions when they face pressures from the organization. Describing the way the competitive environment contributes to these pressures, elsewhere Vaughan (1983) pointed out that society's definition of success results in new goals being set whenever individuals meet the goals set by themselves or their organization. Essentially, aspirations are never ending, and frustration is likely to occur at some point. This is related to Wheeler and his associates' (1988b) fear of falling explanation for white-collar crime. They pointed out that some individuals become successful by being patient and persevering. Once they attain their goals, a threat to their lifestyle may arise, and they do things to make sure that their lifestyle remains intact and their goals remain fulfilled.

Coleman's (1994) culture of competition theory also has ties to Merton's typology. Coleman characterized the U.S. culture as a competitive society in which values such as greed, lust for power, and ego gratification are encouraged. The competitive culture rewards upper-class individuals who find ways to advance their economic success, whether the strategies are legitimate or illegitimate. According to Coleman (1994: 196) defining "wealth and success as the central goals of individual economic activity" creates a society where one would expect white-collar crime to flourish.

Similar assumptions are found in Steven Messner and Richard Rosenfeld's (2001) *Crime and the American Dream.* The source of crime, according to Messner and Rosenfeld, are the kinds of values that are taught in the pursuit of the American dream. These values (e.g., achievement orientation, individualism, and fetishism of money) motivate some individuals to do whatever it takes to achieve financial success (Simon & Hagan, 1999). Though Messner and Rosenfeld (2001) give relatively little attention to explaining how their theory relates to white-collar crime (they apply it more to conventional crime), it is telling to note that they begin their manuscript by highlighting Michael Milken's legal troubles as an illustration of the American dream gone astray. Describing why they believed

Milken became the junk bond king of the 1980s, they wrote:

> The very qualities in which Milken took pride and for which he was praised—his daring, energy, intelligence, and most important, his ability to create and willingness to use innovative solutions for conventional problems—also led to his crimes and punishment. These qualities are not merely the personal traits of a particular criminal (or "economic reformer"); they are elements of a social character rooted in broad value orientations within American culture. (p. 2)

Thus, Messner and Rosenfeld see the values that coincide with goals calling for "success at any cost" as the root cause of crime.

Robert Agnew's (1985, 1992) general strain theory also builds on Merton's typology to explain the cause of crime. Taking a social-psychological approach to explain crime, Agnew sees crime as an adaptation to stress and frustration. Agnew described three types of psychological strain that could result in crime. First, *failure to achieve positively valued goals* occurs when one is unable to attain an aspiration that society, or the organization, defines as positive. Certainly, white-collar offenders who commit crimes against their business because they didn't get the raise or promotion they wanted would, from Agnew's perspective, be responding to the failure to achieve goals. Second, *removal or expected removal of positively valued stimuli* describes the strain that arises when individuals experience, or expect to experience, the loss of something held valuable to the individual. Wheeler and colleagues' (1988b) characterization of white-collar offenders who commit crime because they have a "fear of falling" and losing their lifestyle are examples of those who commit white-collar crimes because of the expected removal of positively valued stimuli. Third, *confronting or expecting to confront negative stimuli* entails the confrontation of negative events in individuals' lives. Instances where upper level management pressure workers to commit crimes (See Clinard, 1983) would be an example of the way that negative stimuli contribute to white-collar crime.

Of course all of these different stress/strain explanations confront a number of criticisms. One of the most commonly heard criticisms is that a lot of people experience stress, but not everyone commits criminal acts as a result of the stress (Green, 1997; Payne, 2000). Despite this criticism, it is most likely that some white-collar offenders truly committed their offenses because they could not handle the pressures that were being placed on them. As with the other motivations for white-collar crime, the stress explanation has important implications for corrections professionals who are supervising white-collar offenders. Specifically, offenders who respond to stress by committing white-collar crimes need to learn (1) coping mechanisms and (2) definitions of success that are not based on money. No pun intended, but these areas could be "stressed" during the correctional supervision of white-collar offenders.

GREED

As indicated in Chapter 1, a number of individuals attribute white-collar crime to greed. In fact, there is empirical support for the greed/white-collar crime relationship (Benson, 1985a; Conley, 2000; Daly, 1989; Wheeler, 1992). Greed can be a factor in some white-collar crimes but is certainly not the cause of all white-collar crimes. When greed is a factor, it is believed that the offender's "overriding desire to achieve material things at all costs led [him or her] to commit crimes" (Miller, 1993: 22).

To fully understand how greed may contribute to some white-collar offenses, the difference between "needs" and "greed" is fundamental. Braithwaite (1992: 84) provided a clear distinction between the two kinds of motivations:

1. Needs "are socially constructed as wants that can be satisfied."
2. Greed "is distinguished as a want that can never be satisfied: success is ever-receding, having more leads to wanting more again."

In many ways, those who attribute recent increases in white-collar crime to the 2001 recession are suggesting that these offenses are caused by the need to maintain a constant level of income and that the commission of the offenses represent an attempt to satisfy monetary desires.

Based on the "need-versus-greed" explanations, Braithwaite (1992) cite four motivations for crime:

1. The desire for goods to use.

2. The fear of losing goods that would be used to fulfill a need.
3. A desire for goods for exchange.
4. A fear of losing goods for exchange.

Braithwaite further contended that the first two motivations are more common among conventional criminals and the latter two are more applicable to white-collar crime.

Of course, Braithwaite is not simply talking about greed, and as noted in Chapter 1, greed oversimplifies the actual cause of many types of white-collar crime (Glasberg & Skidmore, 1998). Also, some say that there is a difference between greed and living beyond one's means, and that white-collar offenders are more apt to live beyond their means (Breed, 1979). Even so, the possibility that greed contributes to living beyond one's means has important implications for correctional officials who supervise white-collar offenders. Specifically, if supervised offenders continue to demonstrate values that would seem to be consistent with greed, it would be worthwhile to direct efforts toward getting white-collar offenders to reassess their real priorities in life.

GAMBLING AND WHITE-COLLAR CRIME

Gambling problems are also seen as a source of many white-collar offenses. Anecdotal evidence suggests a clear relationship between gambling and white-collar crime. For instance, Wright (2001) described an offender who stole $7.75 million from his company as a way to pay off his $36-million-dollar gambling debt that had accumulated over just one year. Some offenders are quick to cite gambling as playing a role in their offenses. Weisburd and Waring (2001: 70) quoted an offender who said:

> I began to get a bit of a big head and living beyond my means along with
> a little bit of gambling. I began realizing what was happening, and started
> borrowing money to get out of debt, intending fully to repay the loans, but
> at the same time my earnings began dropping which led me to bankrupt-
> cy and the trouble I am in now.

For those who see gambling as an actual cause of criminal behavior, there is a belief that gambling can actually be an addiction or a disease in the same way that alcoholics suffer from a disease. Psychiatrists refer to this condition as pathological gambling, which is defined in the following way:

> A chronic and progressive failure to resist impulses to gamble and gambling behavior that comprises, disrupts, or damages personal, family, or vocational pursuits. The gambling preoccupation, urge, and activity increase during periods of stress. Problems that arise as a result of the gambling lead to an intensification of the gambling behavior. Characteristic problems include extensive indebtedness and consequent default on debts and other financial responsibilities, disrupted family relationships, inattention to work, and financially motivated illegal activities to pay for gambling (*Diagnostic and Statistical Manual of Mental Disorders*, 4th Edition, pp. 324-325).

It is further believed that those who suffer from pathological gambling will go through a series of stages that initiate them into the addiction, escalate, and eventually run the gambler's life. These stages are outlined in Table 2.4.

TABLE 2.4
STAGES OF COMPULSIVE GAMBLING

Stage	Behavior
Stage One	Developing a tolerance for gambling
Stage Two	Developing an intolerance for losing
Stage Three	Preoccupation with gaming
Stage Four	Lack of concern for consequences of gambling or illegal actions
Stage Five	Withdrawal Symptoms
Stage Six	Slips and relapses
Stage Seven	Cross-addiction (smoking, caffeine, alcohol)

Source: Final Report of the Task Force on Gambling Addiction in Maryland, 1990.

Four points about these stages are noteworthy in the area of white-collar crime explanations. First, a lack of concern about the consequences of behavior has been commonly tied to white-collar criminals in general, regardless of whether they have a gambling addiction. Second, the intolerance with losing goes hand in hand with the possibility that pathological white-collar gamblers who lose will experience stress, which as already noted, may also contribute to white-collar crime. Third, many of these stages (lack of concern, intolerance, etc.) go hand and hand with the kinds of characteristics one would expect from those who have a low self-control. Not surprisingly, Gottfredson and Hirschi (1990) saw excessive gambling as an indicator of a low self-control. Fourth, though some say that gambling causes white-collar crime, others argue that we must ask what causes the gambling before accurately understanding the cause of white-collar crime.

A number of individuals think the gambling/white-collar crime relationship could be overstated. At one point, estimates attributed to a study by the American Insurance Institute claimed that 40 percent of white-collar crimes were caused by compulsive gambling. However, the American Insurance Institute does not exist, and no research has ever supported this 40 percent estimate though it is widely cited (Fahrenkopf, 1997).

To determine whether a relationship between casino gambling and white-collar crime exists, Albanese (1999) examined the trends of three white-collar offenses (embezzlement, forgery, and fraud) in nine cities with casinos and two cities without casinos. He found that single factors in and of themselves did not cause white-collar crime. Instead, he suggested that the way individuals define the problems they confront was the primary cause of white-collar offending. Using prior white-collar crime explanations as a guide, Albanese suggested that those who see problems as "nonshareable" or who fear their family will suffer from past choices are those who are more likely to turn to white-collar misconduct.

Although gambling is not necessarily a major cause of a majority of white-collar crimes, the gambling/white-collar crime relationship that does exist, though small, still has implications for corrections professionals who supervise white-collar offenders. On the one hand, if a white-collar offender truly exhibits characteristics that are consistent with what would be expected of pathological gambling, then measures would need to be taken to help the offender deal with the gambling problem. Possible measures include gambler's anonymous, group counseling, or individual treatment helping the offender to overcome the addiction. On the other hand, even if gambling isn't the root cause of white-collar crime, as Albanese suggested, the phrase "nonshareable financial problem" implies that the offender's pride has prohibited him or her from communicating with others that he or she has developed a problem. This suggests that corrections professionals should focus on ways to enhance white-collar offender's interpersonal communication skills with significant others.

DRUG ABUSE AND WHITE-COLLAR CRIME

There are also those who suggest that drug abuse causes white-collar crime. Drug abuse is believed to influence white-collar crime in one of two ways. First, there is a belief that substance abuse reduces people's inhibitions, thereby causing some to commit crimes at work if they are under the influence at work. Second, there is a belief that substance abuse becomes an expensive habit forcing some white-collar employees to turn to white-collar crime as a way to deal with their habit. As with the gambling/white-collar crime relationship, anecdotal evidence tends to support this possibility. Explained former white-collar inmate turned prison consultant Ron Cohen, "Alcohol made me feel like I was bulletproof. So I kept making the same dumb choices over and over again" (Cutter, 2001: 194).

There is indirect empirical evidence that some white-collar offenders may commit their offenses, in part, due to substance abuse. For instance, a study of convicted white-collar offenders found that drug use is a predictor of recidivism in the short term (Weisburd et al., 1993). In a separate study, Weisburd and Waring (2001) found that one in five chronic white-collar offenders (e.g., those who were arrested three or more times) had substance abuse problems. As with gambling, though drug abuse does not necessarily explain all white-collar misconduct, it may explain some of the misdeeds committed by white-collar offenders.

For correctional professionals, it is likely not surprising that a relationship exists between drug abuse and white-collar offending. The vast majority of offenders under correctional supervision have substance abuse problems, and a significant minority of white-collar offenders may as well. The key point correctional professionals should keep in mind is that not all white-collar offenders will require substance abuse treatment, but some will.

DENIALS

According to a number of criminologists, another reason that white-collar offenses occur is due to the fact that white-collar offenders are able to deny their actions and justify them as appropriate. The notion of denial has received a great deal of attention from academics and the media alike. Because denial ties directly to the ability to ignore the consequences of white-collar offending, and because there are many different kinds of denial, the way that denials contribute to white-collar crime will be considered in the next chapter in conjunction with the actual consequences of white-collar crime.

CONCLUDING REMARKS

Several different motivations for white-collar crime have been suggested in this chapter. Two points are critical to understanding the motivations of white-collar crime. First, it is important to realize that motivations vary from offender to offender and offense to offense. As an illustration, Weisburd and Waring (2001: 64) cite four kinds of white-collar offenders by distinguishing among the motivations for the offense. First, *crisis responders* are low frequency offenders who face a crisis and take advantage of the trust they have been afforded as a means to deal with the crisis. Second, *opportunity takers* are low frequency offenders who have occasional desires to "take advantage of some specific criminal opportunity. Third, *opportunity seekers* are more frequent offenders who vigorously look for the opportunity to commit white-collar offenses. Finally, *stereotypical criminals* are white-collar offenders who commit an assortment of white-collar offenses in addition to committing conventional crimes. According to Weisburd and Waring (2001), stereotypical criminals have a history of instability and low self-control. Whether one agrees with their classification scheme or not, it is virtually impossible to argue against the suggestion that motivations vary among offenders.

Second, it is equally important to stress that these various motivations often work in conjunction with one another. This means that the offender may have multiple motivations for committing the misconduct. For instance, an individual with a low self-control may have a drug problem and a gambling problem that causes the offender to steal from his or her workplace to support both habits. To address the fact that multiple motivations may contribute to white-collar crime, some criminologists have offered integrated explanations as a basis for understanding why white-collar crime occurs.

In fact, one of the first explanations of embezzling coming out of Cressey's (1953) interviews with 300 incarcerated embezzlers suggested that embezzling occurred as a result of a combination of three elements: (1) a motive such as an unshareable financial problem, (2) a perceived opportunity to offend, and (3) the availability of excuses (Wells, 1990). In a similar integrative fashion, Benson and Moore (1992) argued that white-collar crime is caused by "both opportunities and motives generated by macro social, economic, and organizational processes, which create paths or routes to white-collar crime."

In other words, social forces beyond the individual may play a role in pushing certain individuals into white-collar offending. This is not to suggest that offenders should not be held accountable for their misconduct; rather it is to suggest that motivations for white-collar crime can be influenced by extenuating factors. Likewise, motivations to stay free from white-collar crime can also be influenced by extenuating factors. One possible extenuating factor is appropriate intervention and supervision of white-collar offenders by corrections officials.

APPLIED CRITICAL THINKING QUESTIONS

1. Why is it important for corrections professionals to understand the motivations for white-collar misconduct?
2. If by their very nature white-collar employers are so rational, why is it that they commit crime?
3. How would the learning of white-collar crime be different from the learning of conventional types of crime?
4. What does self-control have to do with white-collar crime?
5. What kinds of stress might influence individuals to commit crime in the workplace?
6. How does greed contribute to white-collar crime? What does this mean for corrections professionals?

7. Are drugs and gambling important factors in explaining white-collar crime? Explain.
8. How do the motivations discussed in this chapter relate to one another? How are they different?
9. How could these theories be used to prevent white-collar crime?

Chapter 3

TRUTH AND CONSEQUENCES: DENIAL, EXCUSES, JUSTIFICATIONS AND WHITE-COLLAR CRIME CONSEQUENCES

INTRODUCTION

Truth or Consequences was a popular game show on television from 1956 until 1974. The appeal of the game was based on its structure: Contestants were asked a rather tricky question by the host, the most popular of whom was Bob Barker. The question was usually so difficult that the contestant was not able to answer. Beulah the Buzzer would go off, and Bob Barker would tell the contestants that since they failed to tell the truth, they would have to pay the consequences. The consequences were usually of an embarrassing or amusing nature. Hence, the name of the game—*Truth or Consequences.*

The phrase "truth or consequences" has direct bearing on the nature of white-collar crime. Specifically, one of the common explanations for white-collar crime is that offenders are able to convince themselves and others that their behavior is appropriate (e.g., they deny the truth), and that their actions have no serious consequences on anyone (e.g., supposedly no one got hurt). Consider the following cases:

- A founder of an alternative school was sentenced to prison for sixty-five months after he falsified attendance records allowing his school to be overpaid $42,000 in state funds. He claimed that he falsified the records in order to "get sufficient funding" to provide an education to the students (Doege, 2001: 03B). As a result of his actions, other schools were deprived of funding.

- One doctor defrauded Medicaid of several thousand dollars by charging for more extensive services than he actually provided. He justified his actions on the grounds that Medicaid's reimbursement rates were too low and no one was being hurt by the overbillings (Rosoff et al., 1998). As a result of actions such as these, individuals who need health care are deprived of it (Pontell et al., 1982).

- Three financial officers stole $2.6 million from the Monmouth Medical Center in Long Branch, New Jersey, by billing for supplies that were never received, stealing supplies and selling them on the open market, and laundering the fraudulently obtained money through fake bank accounts. Their reasoning—after receiving a less than satisfactory bonus, one of them said, "We kind of felt cheated or beat out of some money; we wanted to get our fair share of the pot" (Sandrik, 1993: 35). Among other things, as a result of their actions, the price of everyone's health care increased.

In each of these cases, the offenders were convinced that their behavior was appropriate, justified, and perhaps even harmless. To illustrate the way rationalizations influence white-collar crime and establish that there are indeed important consequences that arise as the result of misconduct on the job, this chapter considers the notions of denials, excuses, and justifications; their functions; the traditional types of each; how they relate to white-collar crime; and the actual consequences of their behavior. Tied throughout the discussion are comments showing that these denials, excuses, justifications, and their consequences have important implications for the handling of white-collar offenders who are under some form of correctional supervision.

FUNCTIONS OF DENIALS AND RATIONALIZATIONS

When individuals do things that they know are inappropriate, it is common for them to either deny or rationalize their misconduct. Some readers may recall the following exchange between two characters in *The Big Chill*:

"It occurs to me that what you just said is a load of rationalizations."

"Don't put down rationalizations, most people can't get through the day without a couple of juicy rationalizations, they're more important than sex."
"That's crazy!"
"Oh, yeah? When's the last time you went for a week without a rationalization?"

Technically speaking, denial occurs when individuals indicate that they did not perform the act in question whereas rationalizations (aka neutralizations) occur when individuals offer excuses for their misconduct. It not just common for individuals to deny or rationalize their misconduct, some would say that it is both natural and functional. In fact, denials and rationalizations serve at least five functions. These functions and how they arise are outlined in Table 3.1.

TABLE 3.1
FUNCTIONS OF DENIAL

Function	Example
Behavioral drifting	Most white-collar offenders are rational offenders who know right from wrong. Given that they know the appropriate behaviors, they must rationalize their behavior in order to allow them to drift into behaviors that violate societal norms.
Intrinsic identity maintenance	Denials and rationalizations allow individuals to continue to see themselves in a relatively positive light.
Extrinsic identity maintenance	Denials and rationalizations allow individuals to avoid the shame that comes along with spoiled identities.
Avoidance of punishment	When taken to the extreme, denials and rationalizations may help white-collar offenders to avoid punishment, or at the very least, minimize the punishment they would otherwise receive.
Continued drifting	Denials and rationalizations allow offenders to maximize their offenses by giving them the fortitude to continue their misconduct.

One function of denials and rationalizations that has ties to the criminological literature is what the author refers to as *behavioral drifting*. More often than not, when individuals think of denials and rationalizations, they tend to think of comments individuals make after performing some illicit act. Some criminologists, however, argue that many offenders may rationalize their behavior prior to committing an act, and that the rationalization allows individuals to commit the misconduct (Sykes & Matza, 1957). In *Delinquency and Drift*, David Matza (1964) took this idea a step further and argues that neutralizations allow individuals to drift into and out of law violations.

With regard to white-collar crime, behavioral drifting is particularly likely because most white-collar offenders are rational beings who know the rules and standards of society. As well, for the majority of their lives, white-collar offenders have abided by societal norms. In order for them to do things they know are wrong, they must deny or rationalize their conduct. After their denial or rationalization, their behavior can drift into the misconduct. Then, the denial and rationalization allows them to drift back into the identity of a useful citizen rather than the identity of a miscreant. This relates to a second function of denials and rationalizations.

In particular, denials and rationalizations by white-collar offenders allow them to maintain a positive self-image (Covington, 1984). The author refers to this function as *intrinsic identity maintenance* because the benefits of the denial are within the individual offender. By denying or rationalizing the offense, offenders do not define themselves as criminals, thereby allowing them to manage their identities in ways consistent with their expectations. As Hamlin (1988: 436) pointed out, "The guilt individuals . . . feel after being told that what they did was wrong or that they themselves are bad can be destructive of the social identity. [Denials and rationalizations] neutralize guilt and allow individuals to continue to feel good about themselves."

A third and related function of denials and rationalizations is *extrinsic identity maintenance*. This has to do with the fact that individuals use denials and rationalizations to manipulate the way that they are seen by others. Described as a performance by Goffman (1959), individuals will do things so their audience sees them in positive terms. Denials and rationalizations are among the repertoire used in performances designed to hide shameful events. Managing their identities in positive ways increases the likelihood that individuals are accepted by others (Goffman, 1963).

Another function of denials and rationalizations is that they help offenders to avoid the various sanctions that would be imposed on them should they immediately admit guilt (Covington, 1984). Denials and rationalizations can influence punishment in one of three ways: (1) they may eliminate the possibility that a sanction is imposed; (2) they may delay the imposition of punishment; or (3) they may reduce the levity of the sanction imposed on the offender. If the offender continues to deny guilt and the state cannot prove guilt, then formal sanctions are eliminated. If the offender denies guilt until a plea bargain is offered, then the imposition of the punishment is both delayed and reduced.

A final function of rationalizations and denials is that the strategies allow for continued drifting into and out of behaviors that go against conventional norms. Keep in mind that most white-collar offenders, especially those who have been incarcerated, did not commit just one white-collar crime; rather they have committed several criminal acts. The denials and rationalizations allow them to maintain dual roles as (1) valued white-collar employees who appear to deserve the trust they are afforded, and (2) white-collar offenders who have, in their minds, legitimate reasons to commit their offenses.

Denials and rationalizations have received a great deal of attention from criminologists. Sutherland was one of the first to note the importance of rationalizations and did so in the fourth principle of his theory of differential association (e.g., "learning includes . . . the specific direction of motives, drives, rationalizations, and attitudes"). Nearly two decades after Sutherland first presented this theory, Gresham Sykes and David Matza (1957) took this aspect from the fourth principle and described what they called *techniques of neutralization.*

Sykes and Matza's Techniques of Neutralization

During the 1950s, the prevailing belief among criminologists was that individuals committed delinquent or criminal acts because they were a part of a criminal or delinquent subculture that held values opposing those of conventional society. Sykes and Matza (1957) challenged this assumption and contended that the majority of individuals had a similar set of values that would allow most individuals to know right from wrong. The task, then, they noted was to explain why individuals who held conventional values would violate societal standards of conduct. According to Sykes and Matza, the reason why those individuals violated the law was that they used a neutralization process that at least temporarily disassociated individuals from conventional norms and values. Once their behavior was neutralized, individuals had the capacity to violate the law.

To explain this neutralization process, Sykes and Matza described five major types of neutralization:

1. The *denial of responsibility* entails instances where individuals convince themselves that there are factors beyond their control influencing their decision to violate the law. This allows criminals to see themselves as responding to an action rather than as an active law violator.
2. The *denial of injury* involves instances where criminals convince themselves that no one will be harmed by their actions.
3. The *denial of victim* entails the contention that those who get harmed from the individual's actions deserve the consequences they experience.
4. The *condemnation of condemners* is a neutralization technique whereby the offender justifies his or her actions on the grounds that those who would blame the offender for wrongdoing are also wrongdoers themselves.
5. *Appeal to higher loyalties* occurs when individuals justify their misconduct on the grounds that the malfeasance is for the benefit of a group to whom the law violator is loyal.

These techniques have been used by a number of criminologists to explain different types of criminal behavior, and are especially applicable to explaining white-collar crime (Dabney, 1995; Hollinger, 1991). Table 3.2 provides an overview of the way that each neutralization applies to white-collar crime. What follows is a description of the way each neutralization relates to different aspects of white-collar crime with specific attention given to the implications each neutralization has for corrections professionals.

TABLE 3.2
SYKES AND MATZA'S NEUTRALIZATIONS AND WHAT THEY
MEAN TO CORRECTIONS

Neutralization	Example	Implications
Denial of responsibility	• Forces beyond my control caused me to steal $300,000 from my company. • I'm a drug addict.	Individuals need to take responsibility for their actions to become empowered and able to control future behavior.
Denial of victim	• The company deserved what I did to it because they had no concern for my well-being. • I was never paid enough for my blood, sweat, and tears. They owed it to me.	Individuals who show little remorse may have problems restoring themselves to a functional level once they are released from correctional supervision.
Denial of injury	• So, I stole from the government. Nobody got hurt! • My company makes billions a year. They won't miss a few thousand dollars here and there.	Unless they see that their actions have a range of consequences, individuals who fail to see the true consequences of their behavior may continue reckless actions when they are released from supervision.
Condemnation of condemners	• The criminal justice system is out to get me to make an example of me. • My boss set me up.	Blaming the system suggests the offender will see his or her punishment as particularly unwarranted, and because punishment felt as too severe may contribute to future crimes, the offender will need to see that (a) the punishment fits the offense and (b) others are also being placed under correctional supervision for similar offenses.
Appeal to higher loyalties	• If I hadn't done this, the company would have gone under. • My family needed me to do this. • If I hadn't done this, these customers would not have gotten the services they needed.	These individuals my be particularly loyal to their place of work or their family. Their ability to be loyal suggests that they can also become loyal in more appropriate and functional ways.

First, it is common to hear white-collar offenders claim that they are not responsible for their actions. One woman, for instance, "admitted she encountered financial troubles while employed and found her access to the business' financial materials too great to resist" (Doege, 2001: 03B). Other white-collar offenders have claimed that they are not responsible because of factors beyond their control such as drug addiction, gambling problems, and financial troubles. According to Harrington (1996), those who tend to deny responsibility can be deterred if they are provided with clear guidelines or policies about what is expected from them. This suggests that corrections professionals can help white-collar criminals to remain crime free by making sure that they understand that they are responsible for their actions, and that there are specific rules to which offenders will be expected to abide on release.

Regarding denial of injury, it is also common to hear of white-collar offenders believing that no one is harmed by the workplace misconduct. For example, insider traders often justify their actions by suggesting that no one was hurt by their sharing of information. After all, those who receive the useful information are sure to benefit from the knowledge (Schroeder & Barrett, 1996). Other white-collar criminals justify their crimes against the workplace by suggesting that the company is not being harmed because it has insurance to cover any losses incurred from theft (Conley, 2000). Because some white-collar criminals deny that individuals are hurt from their actions, it will be up to corrections professionals to convince the supervised offenders that there are consequences from their misconduct.

As far as denial of victim is concerned, there are certainly instances where white-collar offenders suggest that the victim deserved the harm they suffered. One offender blamed the lax bookkeeping system of her employer for her pilfering the company's profits. Had they not made it so easy for her, she reasoned, she would not have embezzled the million dollars (Franzen, 2001). Another white-collar offender justified stealing $1.1 million from a record company with the following comment, "In my mind, I thought I would be rewarded for extra work based on promises [my boss] made" (Kircher, 1997: 1). As another example, a doctor defended his physical abuse of patients by stating that "he never turned away Medicaid patients—even though many of them are 'dirty' and 'smell bad'" (Rosoff et al., 1998: 333).

Denial of victim is basically the same as blaming the victim for the misdeeds. Blaming the victim tends to mask the real issues and the real problems. Unfortunately, society also tends to blame victims for misconduct, thus providing offenders the opportunity to use this neutralization (Cullen et al., 1983). It is important that corrections professionals help supervised white-collar offenders develop a sense of empathy for those they harmed. Otherwise, the likelihood that offenders will continue their misconduct when they are released increases.

One can also readily see how white-collar offenders utilize the appeal to higher loyalties neutralization. Gibson (2000: 67) remarked, "Authority as a motivator is so strong that it often exerts its influence without any explicit orders." In terms of white-collar crime, this means that individuals will do things, or at least say they do things, because they were responding to their bosses' orders. Indirectly citing this neutralization, one white-collar offender remarked, "my crime was taking money, not for my personal benefit, but for the benefit of others to keep the firm going" (Bennetto, 1998: 9). As another illustration, referred to as the "good soldier defense," some investment brokers claim that they committed their misdeeds in order to "keep analysts and shareholders happy" (Reason, 2000: 112). In terms of implications for corrections professionals supervising white-collar offenders, it is reasonable to suggest that those who use this neutralization have the capacity to show their loyalty to groups. The trick will be to show them how to show their loyalty in more acceptable ways.

Some white-collar offenders will also "condemn their condemners." Those white-collar offenders using this neutralization generally see "the system" as being corrupt. For example, an offender convicted of political corruption once said, "I would like to say that I believe there aren't 535 members of Congress out there who are violating FEC rules. But . . . I can't say that. The system needs to change" (Semerad, 1998: n.p.). Those who condemn condemners usually justify their own offense on the grounds that white-collar crime is a common occurrence in a society that allows these kinds of acts to flourish (Mokhiber, 1988). The task at hand for corrections professionals is to show white-collar offenders that (1) there are honest professionals in "the system," (2) their punishment fits their offense, and (3) others are also being punished for similar offenses.

A number of criticisms have been levied against Sykes and Matza's neutralization theory. The most common criticisms are in the areas of temporal ordering and concerns about the assumption that most individuals buy into conventional norms of society. Regarding the temporal-ordering concerns, not everyone is convinced that neutralizations happen before the act because there is a possibility that the neutralizations are actually excuses or justifications developed after the crime as a means to deny guilt (Agnew & Peters, 1986; Hamlin, 1988). As far as conventional values are concerned, some authors do not believe that the conventional values are accepted by the majority of the population (Minor, 1981; Sheley, 1980).

Despite these criticisms, Sykes and Matza's theory has widespread appeal in criminology and is particularly applicable to white-collar offending. In fact, white-collar offenders are susceptible to using neutralizations for at least three reasons. First, because the majority of white-collar offenders are rational beings, many of them need to rationalize their misconduct in order to see it as appropriate (see Minor, 1981). Second, because most white-collar offenders have accepted the conventional values of society, they would have to find appropriate reasons to violate their own accepted norms and values. Third, research shows that neutralizations are more likely to be used by older offenders (Hollinger, 1991), and given that white-collar offenders are generally older than other offenders, it logically follows that they would be more inclined to use these rationalizations. Indeed, there is a belief that some individuals are socialized to make excuses for behavior that goes against societal standards. (For a rather interesting take on excuses, Table 3.3 lists some rationalizations offered by professional athletes for their misdeeds.)

The widespread appeal of Sykes and Matza's approach is further evidenced by the number of studies that have tested or expanded some aspect of their theory. Not surprisingly, a number of other neutralizations, denials, excuses, and justifications for white-collar crime have been cited in the academic literature. These are discussed in the next section.

TABLE 3.3
STRANGE DENIALS BY ATHLETES: DIFFERENT REASONS USED BY
PROFESSIONAL ATHLETES TO EXPLAIN THEIR ALLEGED MISCONDUCT

Comment	Type of Rationalization	Who said it?
Don't forget, I'm 60 years old.	Denial of Responsibility	Former Dallas Cowboys football coach Barry Switzer on how he forgot that he had a loaded gun on him while going through airport security.
I was harassed by the police, the whole nine yards.	Condemnation of Condemners	Cincinnati Bengals running back Corey Dillon–arrested for driving under the influence, driving with a suspended license, running over a curb, and refusing a field sobriety test and a blood-alcohol test.
I didn't do any. It was just the significant amount of time that I spend (around) marijuana users.	Denial of Fact	Canadian Snowboarder Ross Rebagliati's explanation for testing positive for marijuana after winning the Gold Medal at the Nagano Olympics.
They were flimsy, anyway. All you had to do was sit on them, and they'd break.	Denial of Victim	Olympic hockey player Jeremy Roenick, describing chairs destroyed after the U.S. hockey team trashed three rooms at the Nagano Olympics.
This is the greatest travesty I've ever seen.	Condemnation of Condemners	Former Indiana University basketball coach Bobby Knight on being kicked out of a game after a long shouting match with the referee.
Even if I did do this, it would have to have been because I loved her very much, right?	Appeal to Higher Loyalties	O.J. Simpson, in response to allegations that he killed his former wife, Nicole Brown Simpson, and her friend, Ron Goldman. He is tacitly suggesting love is a higher loyalty than life.
That's my story and I'm sticking to it.	Denial of Denial	Former NFL player Alex Hawkins who told his wife he fell asleep on the hammock on his back porch while he was actually out drinking until 6 a.m. He used this response when his wife told him she had gotten rid of the hammock two weeks earlier.

Source: Adapted from Reilly, R. 1998.

ACCOUNTING FOR BEHAVIOR: DENIALS, EXCUSES, AND JUSTIFICATIONS

When individuals are asked to describe their actions, what they tend to offer is what sociologists refer to as accounts. Accounts are also known as impression management techniques because accounts are typically offered as a way to control the way individuals are seen by others (Tata, 2000). When individuals describe their deviant behaviors, they generally use denials, excuses, or justifications as impression management techniques (Scott & Lyman, 1968; Tata, 2000). Denials are comments suggesting that the individual did not commit the misconduct, or has no knowledge about the misconduct. Excuses are comments in which individuals admit they did something wrong, but fail to accept full responsibility for their actions. Justifications are comments in which offenders accept responsibility for their actions but do not admit wrongdoing. Recall that some criminologists see these accounts as arising before the misconduct whereas others see them as part of a "vocabulary of motives" that arise when individuals are forced to explain themselves (Scott & Lyman, 1968). Regardless of when they arise, each type of account relates to white-collar crime in that many offenders will either deny, justify, or offer excuses for their workplace offenses. The way that denials, excuses, and justifications relate to white-collar crime and their implications for corrections professionals is outlined in Table 3.4.

DENIAL AND WHITE-COLLAR CRIME

Denials occur when individuals suggest that they did not commit the act in question or they deny that they have knowledge about the act in question. Denials are particularly useful for white-collar criminals because they keep the offenders from actually defining themselves as criminals (Benson, 1985a). There are at least five types of denials offered by white-collar offenders.

First, *denial of crime* is the most straightforward type of denial, and it occurs when offenders suggest that they did not commit the crime. Research shows that white-collar criminals convicted of fraud are among the most likely to deny committing the act in question

TABLE 3.4
THE CONTINUUM OF ACCOUNTS: DENIAL, EXCUSES, AND JUSTIFICATIONS AND THEIR IMPLICATIONS FOR CORRECTIONS PROFESSIONALS

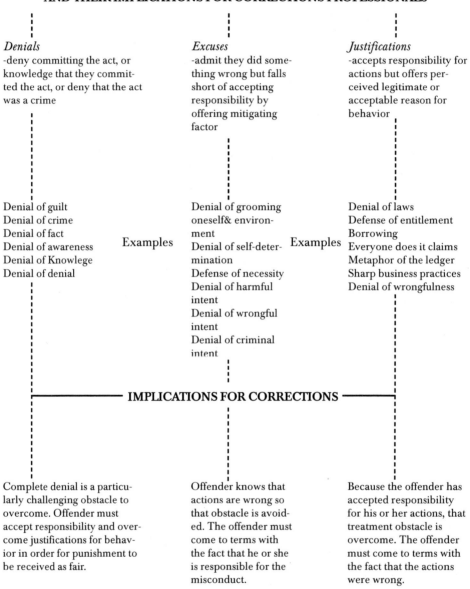

Denials	*Excuses*	*Justifications*
-deny committing the act, or knowledge that they committed the act, or deny that the act was a crime	-admit they did something wrong but falls short of accepting responsibility by offering mitigating factor	-accepts responsibility for actions but offers perceived legitimate or acceptable reason for behavior
Denial of guilt Denial of crime Denial of fact Denial of awareness **Examples** Denial of Knowlege Denial of denial	Denial of grooming oneself& environment Denial of self-deter- **Examples** mination Defense of necessity Denial of harmful intent Denial of wrongful intent Denial of criminal intent	Denial of laws Defense of entitlement Borrowing Everyone does it claims Metaphor of the ledger Sharp business practices Denial of wrongfulness

———— IMPLICATIONS FOR CORRECTIONS ————

Complete denial is a particularly challenging obstacle to overcome. Offender must accept responsibility and overcome justifications for behavior in order for punishment to be received as fair.	Offender knows that actions are wrong so that obstacle is avoided. The offender must come to terms with the fact that he or she is responsible for the misconduct.	Because the offender has accepted responsibility for his or her actions, that treatment obstacle is overcome. The offender must come to terms with the fact that the actions were wrong.

(Benson, 1985a). Those who deny committing any offense whatso-ever will neither accept responsibility or admit wrongdoing because to do so would be an admission of guilt, which would break down their impression management strategy. Many white-collar offenders deny that they committed any crime whatsoever (Eichenwald, 2002).

Second, *denial of guilt* is a more subtle denial in which the offender technically does not reject the idea that he or she committed the act in question, but does deny that the offender is guilty of any wrong-doing. These denials are so common that some have been heard to quip, "There's no such thing as a guilty [white-collar offender]" (Solomon, 1998: 54). During his sentencing hearing, one white-collar criminal said, "I thought that what I was doing was approved, plain and simple" (Jenkins, 2002: 2). Like denial of crime, those who offer this denial will neither admit wrongdoing nor accept responsi-bility for their actions.

Third, *denial of fact* occurs when individuals dispute a particular fact about the misconduct. As an example, a former state attorney general was sentenced to two years in a federal prison after being convicted for misusing state property for political and personal use. He was quick to claim, "I did not put money in my pocket" as a way to dispute the facts of the case that suggested that he directly stole from the state (Ganey, 1994: 01A). With this denial, offenders admit that something happened, they simply deny a particular facet of the behavior–thereby rejecting responsibility and wrongfulness.

Fourth, *denial of awareness*, which could also be denial of knowl-edge, entails instances where offenders suggest that they were not aware that they did anything wrong. It is common for white-collar offenders to utilize this claim. Said one former high school football coach who received $75,000 in what he thought were incentive rais-es and numerous free trips from a fraudulent administrator at the high school: "If I did something wrong. . . . If I'd known–from the bottom of my heart–I never would have done it" (Holland, 2000: n.p.). Like the other denials, this one allows offenders to save face by rejecting responsibility and wrongdoing.

Fifth, *denial of denial* occurs when offenders are questioned about their denials and respond by insisting that they are not denying any-thing (Winn, 1996). Some would say that Congressman Gary Condit's refusal to discuss his involvement with Chandra Levy was a denial of denial. He always insisted that he was being completely up-front with the police in answering all of the questions that were asked of him. The police, on the other hand, contended that the way Condit avoided questions from the media was the same way he responded to the questions from the police. Yet, Condit denied that he was denying anything.

These denials have important implications for corrections professionals supervising white-collar offenders. In particular, offenders who are in complete denial present obstacles that are particularly challenging to overcome. Experts suggest that confrontation is generally not the best way to overcome denial. Specific strategies to overcome denial will be suggested in the treatment section in Chapter 5. For now, it is important to note that many white-collar offenders in denial define themselves as unlucky, but not as individuals who committed a crime (Breed, 1979). Consequently, if they never come to terms with their responsibility or their wrongdoing, they will be inclined to see the system's response as unfair, excessive, and/or unnecessary. Those who see their punishment in this light will be more likely to become hardened as opposed to rehabilitated.

EXCUSES AND WHITE-COLLAR CRIME

Not all white-collar offenders will deny their misconduct. Some will admit that they did something wrong, but will fall short of accepting responsibility for their actions. They will, in effect, make excuses for their misconduct. The following five excuses are particularly common among white-collar offenders:

1. *Denial of grooming oneself and environment*–denies planning the offense, describes it as an accident or a spontaneous event without planning (e.g., "It was an accident," see Winn, 1996).
2. *Denial of self-determination*–claims that something beyond the offender's control forced him or her to commit the offenses ("I learned to be impulsive from my siblings," see Pollock & Hashmall, 1991).
3. *Defense of necessity*–defends actions on the grounds that they had to be taken for some reason (e.g., "I did it for my family,"

see Minor, 1981).

4. *Denial of harmful intent*–claims that no harm was intended from the offender's actions (e.g., "I never intended for anyone to lose money," see Ruth, 2000)

5. *Denial of wrongful intent/denial of criminal intent*–suggests that inappropriate actions were not intended ("I didn't mean to do anything wrong," see Benson, 1985a).

These last two are among the most common excuses offered, in part due to the fact that intent is terribly difficult to prove in white-collar crime cases, and these denials help to insulate offenders from prosecution (Benson, 1985a; Cauther, 2001). Also note that excuses are natural responses we would expect from individuals committed to the conventional order. In fact, drawing on the work of McCaghy (1968), Minor (1981: 311) pointed out that offering excuses can be seen as "an indication of conventional commitment."

Minor's assertion has important implications for corrections professionals supervising white-collar offenders. If excuse making is an indicator of commitment, and the offender knows that he or she did something wrong, then a major obstacle to treatment has been avoided. Given that excuse makers are trying to escape responsibility, efforts would need to be directed towards strategies that would encourage the acceptance of responsibility. Some of these strategies are considered in Chapter 5.

JUSTIFICATIONS AND WHITE-COLLAR CRIME

While some white-collar offenders will either deny or make excuses for their misconduct, others will accept responsibility for their actions but offer comments suggesting that their actions were appropriate under the circumstances in which the act was committed. Or, they will justify their actions. Seven related justifications have been offered by white-collar offenders.

First, *denial of law* is a justification in which offenders suggest that the rules or regulations governing their behavior are just plain unfair (Coleman, 1994). It is common, for instance to hear fraudulent doctors claim that the regulations governing Medicaid reimbursements are inherently unfair (Jesilow et al., 1993). Because they believe the payment system for Medicaid is unfair, they overcharge the Medicaid system. The law, in their minds, is wrong, and their fraudulent actions are justified.

Second, and somewhat related, is the *defense of entitlement* in which offenders justify their workplace offenses on the grounds that they are underpaid, overworked, and underappreciated (Coleman, 1994; Yu, 1998). This justification surfaces when the employee feels resentment towards the employer as a result of the perceived salary problems, lack of respect, and unfair expectations.

White-collar offenders will also justify their misconduct on the grounds that they were *borrowing* the company's property and that they had every intention of paying the company back (Coleman, 1994; Gray, 1997). Consider the following two examples:

1. A judge convicted of tax evasion said that "he didn't take the money, but borrowed it to help pay for college and postgraduate education for his five children" (Apgar, 1999: 1).
2. After defrauding 50 investors out of five million dollars, an offender said, "I really thought I could have worked everything out and paid everyone back" (Behar, 1998: 222).

Borrowing claims allow offenders to maintain their identities by accepting responsibility but deflecting blame by suggesting that they really did not commit a crime, but they borrowed something with every intention of returning it.

A fourth justification offered by white-collar offenders are *claims that everyone steals* from the workplace or commits related workplace offenses (Friedrichs, 1996). In some settings, these claims may actually be accurate. For instance, interviews with 25 registered nurses by criminologist Dean Dabney (1995) revealed that 23 of the nurses admitted stealing supplies, and 21 reported stealing nonnarcotic drugs at some point during their career. Offenders will utilize this claim for one of two reasons: (1) they believe that the behavior will continue whether the offender does it or not, or (2) they adhere to the adage "When in Rome, do as the Romans do" (Gibson, 2000).

Some white-collar offenders will also use a justification referred to as the *metaphor of the ledger*. This justification suggests that an occasional discretion is okay as long as the individual has generally abided to societal rules (Minor, 1981). For white-collar offenders in particular, those who utilize this justification often believe that it is downright normal to violate rules every now and then.

A sixth justification offered by white-collar offenders is that their behavior was not criminal, but was simply *sharp business practices.* Consider a case where twenty employees from a major car rental company stole $13.7 million from 100,000 rental customers by charging the customers full price for auto repairs, while the company actually paid wholesale prices (Koepp, 1988). In their minds, this was simply a smart way to do business. After all, if the customers fixed the autos on their own, they would have had to pay full price anyway. The source of this rationalization, some would argue, is the competitive business culture (Coleman, 1994).

Finally, some white-collar offenders will offer a justification referred to as the *denial of wrongfulness.* This denial entails offenders admitting responsibility but, at the same time, suggesting that there was absolutely nothing wrong with their misdeeds. For example, after being convicted for stealing $1.6 million from 60 elderly investors, one white-collar offender defended his actions stating, "I entered into legal contracts with my clients. I was always honest and straightforward" (Lodge, 2001: 38A). Other white-collar offenders deny wrongfulness when they commit crimes against an organization by claiming that it is not wrong to steal from an organization for the good of individuals. Known as the "Robin Hood Syndrome," offenders will distinguish "between harm done to an organization and harm done to an individual" (Harrington, 1996: 264) and assume that harm to an individual is wrong, whereas harm to an organization is not wrong.

As with denials and excuses, these justifications have important implications for corrections professionals supervising white-collar offenders. Specifically, because the offender has accepted responsibility for his or her actions, then treatment does not have to be directed toward the acceptance of responsibility. However, given that those who justify their actions think they have done nothing wrong, it is important that these offenders come to terms with the fact that their actions were wrong and that there are a number of negative consequences as a result of white-collar misconduct (Smith & Berlin, 1981). Unfortunately, these consequences are often hidden, ignored, and misunderstood. To provide a general understanding of the consequences, the next section addresses the kinds of losses attributed to white-collar crime.

WHITE-COLLAR CRIME CONSEQUENCES

It is extremely difficult to measure the consequences of white-collar crime, but it is generally agreed among criminologists that serious consequences stem from various white-collar offenses. Whereas most conventional crimes target just one or a few victims, one white-collar offense can victimize a large number of victims. As an example, 72-year-old insurance mogul Albert W. Lawrence embezzled $37 million from the government, his companies, his employees, and policy holders. An offense such as this would directly influence hundreds if not thousands of individuals (Furfaro, 2001). In fact, a survey cited by Mokhiber (2000) done by the Training and Research Institute of the National White-Collar Crime Center in Morgantown, West Virginia found that one-third of U.S. households are victims of white-collar crime each year. By these estimates, every household would be victimized by a white-collar offense every three years. The kinds of consequences experienced can be divided into three broad categories—economic costs to society, individual consequences, and trust violations.

Economic Costs to Society

There is no disputing the fact that white-collar offenses cost society enormously in terms of financial losses. In full, it is estimated that society loses $400 billion a year to fraud and abuse (Gray, 1997; Zeune, 2000). This means that the costs of white-collar crime are anywhere from four to five times greater than the costs of conventional crime (see Figure 3.1). For a more specific example, the average bank robbery costs the bank about $3,200 whereas the average embezzlement costs $125,000 (Wells, 1990).

To put these costs into further perspective, experts suggest that revenues would need to increase ten times in order to cover losses to fraud in companies that already have a 10 percent profit margin (Albrecht & Searcy, 2001). Albrecht and Searcy (2001: 58) described what it would take for General Motors to recover its $436 million lost to fraud in the early 1990s: "If GM has a ten percent profit margin, then the company would have to increase revenues by 4.36 billion to compensate for the fraud. This means they'd need to sell 218,000 extra cars." In the end, these societal costs end up affecting everyone. As Moore and Mills (1990: 410) wrote:

FIGURE 3.1. FINANCIAL COSTS OF WHITE-COLLAR CRIME COMPARED TO CONVENTIONAL CRIMES

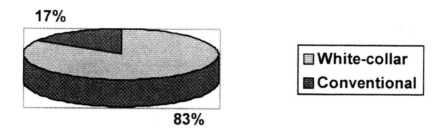

Source: Kappeler (1996).

> Whereas street crimes disproportionately victimize the poor and marginal, white-collar crime is more democratic in its impact. It harms not only well-heeled financial speculators but couples and individuals with few if any assets beyond a modest savings account.

Individual Losses

Individuals are directly influenced by white-collar crime in a variety of ways. Payne (1998) cited three specific types of losses individuals experience as a result of white-collar offenses: physical deprivations, economic deprivations, and time deprivations. Physical deprivations are concerned with the loss of life or physical abilities as a result of white-collar victimization. Injuries from white-collar offenses are not always immediately visible, but they are sure to surface (Moore & Mills, 1990; Schlegel & Weisburd, 1992).

Many criminologists concur that individuals are more likely to be injured or killed by a crime in the workplace than by a conventional crime in any other setting (Friedrichs, 1996). As shown in Figure 3.2, individuals are nearly fifteen times more likely to die from an occupational related offense than from a conventional homicide. Death and physical injuries are not the only physical deprivations experienced by white-collar crime victims. A study by Ganzini and colleagues (1990) found that some victims experienced major depressive orders and generalized anxiety disorders as a result of their victimization. However, these physical consequences are often hidden because some tend to define white-collar crime as nonviolent. Consider the following definition of white-collar crime offered by Turner and Stephenson (1993: 57): "White-collar crimes are those committed without the use or threat of force and without the risk of physical harm to the victim or the criminal." This shallow definition certainly misses the point concerning the actual physical losses experienced by white-collar crime victims.

Individual victims also experience economic deprivations as a result of white-collar crimes. Consider, for instance, the fact that products cost 2 to 5 percent more because of employee fraud (Touby, 1994). This means that everyone loses two to five percent of their spending money as a result of white-collar misconduct. Also note that the individual economic deprivations can be quite large. One victim lost four million dollars when his son-in-law stole from his business (Semerad, 1998). Though most victims do not lose four million dollars, relatively speaking many lose what amounts to be their life savings.

In addition, individual victims will lose an enormous amount of time thinking about the offense, working with the justice system trying to prosecute the offender, and looking for ways to recover their

FIGURE 3.2. NUMBER OF DEATHS EACH YEAR BY DIFFERENT ACTS.

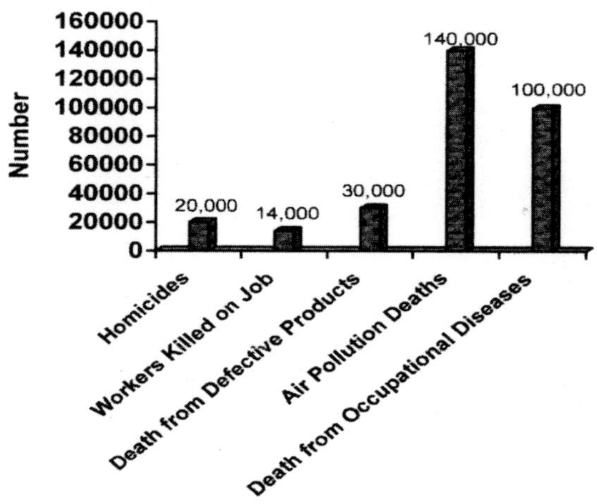

Source: Kappeler, V. (1996).

losses. The reduced standard of living many victims experience only compounds the time losses (Moore and Mills, 1990). White-collar crime victims are forced to change their lifestyle as a result of their victimization, and these changes can be quite time consuming. Certainly, as Szockyj and Frank (1996: 8) told us, white-collar crime "victimization can be clear, substantial, and dramatic in its impact."

Trust Violations and White-Collar Crime

Perhaps one of the most significant consequences of white-collar crime is the erosion of trust that occurs. To some, the violation of trust makes white-collar crime "by far the most heinous of crimes against the consumer" (Claybrook, 1986: 35). Roberts (2000: A02) pointed out that trust "betrayals can be devastating, personally as well as financially." This devastation can be long lasting, with victims feeling betrayed for several years after the misconduct (Shover et al., 1998). Said one victim, "the shock of discovering this betrayal . . . has left a loss and sorrow unmatched in our 90 and 80 plus years of life" (Locy, 1998: PH06). Another white-collar crime victim echoed a similar feeling stating that betrayals affect the whole community: "The thing that bothers me the most about the whole deal is what he did to good family personal relationships and trust in Brady. That will take time to repair" (Ball, 2001: B1).

The trust betrayals are multidimensional in that various aspects of the relationships between individuals, businesses, the government, and society in general are influenced by white-collar crimes. Moore and Mills (1990: 414) cited three ways trust betrayals hinder relationships between individuals and various societal institutions. Specifically, individuals will: (1) witness the gradual destruction of public morality, (2) have less confidence in the political institutions and its members, and (3) have less faith in the business community. As evidence of a reduction in faith, interviews with 142 prospective jurors for an embezzlement trial in which a bank chief executive officer stole $20 million from depositors showed significant erosion in the confidence citizens had toward bankers (*Houston Chronicle*, 1985).

Many businesses will do things to try to minimize the possible loss of faith that consumers would have in the business once a white-collar crime surfaces. Consider the recent offenses involving fixed contests and McDonald's. Jerome P. Jacobsen, an employee of the Georgia-based Simon Marketing, was arrested after he allegedly fixed the outcomes of contests his company was hired to run for McDonald's. Jacobsen gave the winning pieces to a few friends who then recruited others who acted as if they legitimately won the contest. The false winners then provided kickbacks to the other participants (Arena, 2001). When news of the crime first hit the press, McDonald's was quick to go on the offensive to separate itself from this wrongdoing. The company immediately sponsored a new contest to make up for the fraudulent one and gave away millions in an attempt to bolster confidence that consumers had in the company's contests.

The trust violations are not just consequences of white-collar misconduct, they are also a precipitating factor in many of the offenses. This means that some offenders will purposely develop, or use, a trusting relationship as a way to commit their offenses. Consider the following:

- A part-time minister embezzled $1.2 million from three dozen elderly persons he recruited from a Bible study class he led (Fuquay, 2000).
- An investor persuaded three-hundred residents in one community to invest $5 million in businesses that were never developed (Ball 2001).
- A treasurer of an Episcopal church center in New York City stole $2.2 million from the church (Fleckenstein & Bowers, 2000).
- In San Francisco, a reverend stole more than $200,000 from members of his parish (Fleckenstein & Bowers, 2000).

In each of these cases, the trust that was given to the individuals was violated in order to commit the offense. As far as the way that offenders get potential victims to give them trust, con-man-turned-president of a white-collar crime security firm Frank Abagnale had a television station videotape the way he established and violated trust:

> As cameras rolled, the impeccably dressed Abagnale drove up in a Rolls Royce and was escorted by his chauffer. He presented and cashed a check written on a paper napkin. "I would have cashed a check [for him] written on toilet paper" said the teller. (Conlan, 1991: 55)

Clearly, trust is both an element and a consequence of the offense.

It is important that corrections professionals understand the consequences of white-collar offenses for a number of reasons. First, because many individuals do not see these offenses as serious, or white-collar offenders as criminals, it is important that corrections professionals do not fall into the same trap. White-collar offenders are criminals who committed serious offenses that can have grave consequences for society and should be handled accordingly. Second, ignoring the consequences may lead to offenders not receiving the treatment they need, which will increase their likelihood of reoffending. Third, understanding these consequences will help corrections professionals to show offenders who are in denial about their criminality that their actions do have serious consequences. Fourth, in regard to the trust violations specifically, corrections professionals need to understand that some white-collar offenders may try to develop a trusting relationship with the corrections professional not as a means to become rehabilitated, but as a means to dupe professionals and continue in their deviant ways. Recognizing that some of the offenders use trust as a weapon will help professionals to stop that cycle from repeating itself.

CONCLUDING REMARKS

This chapter considered the functions of denials and rationalizations; Sykes and Matza's techniques of neutralizations; the types of denials, excuses, and justifications associated with white-collar crime; and the consequences of white-collar crime. In considering denials and rationalizations, there's no denying that denials and rationalizations happen, the debate centers on when they surface. Some say they arise prior to the misconduct and allow the offender to justify his or her actions while others see them as arising after the misconduct. It is likely the case that denials and rationalizations actually arise throughout the criminal event (e.g., before the crime, during the crime, and after the crime).

Those who see rationalizations as occurring before the criminal act contend that the rationalization does not occur out of the clear blue; instead, a series of events contribute to the offender's decision to rationalize his or her misconduct. Basing his framework on

Cressey's (1953) classic research on embezzlers, Albanese (1999), for instance, cited five stages that eventually lead to an offender rationalizing his or her misconduct (see Table 3.5). First, a financial problem develops in the individual's life. Next, the individual defines or structures the problem as the kind of problem that can not be shared with others. Third, the individual develops a desire to find a quick way to fix the problem. Fourth, the individual finds an opportunity in his or her job to steal to solve the financial problem. Finally, the offender rationalizes his or her misconduct as appropriate or legitimate and then commits the white-collar offense.

One theme that runs through all of the rationalizations is the belief that there are no consequences from the misconduct. As established in this chapter, however, there are serious consequences from all white-collar crimes. Getting back to the "truth and consequences" theme, Bob Barker used to end each episode of *Truth or Consequences* with the statement, "This is Bob Barker, hoping all your consequences are happy ones." Unfortunately, there are few "happy consequences" from white-collar crime. However, if corrections professionals are able to effectively manage and treat white-collar offenders, then perhaps happy consequences will evolve.

APPLIED CRITICAL THINKING QUESTIONS

1. What are the functions of denial?
2. How might white-collar offenders use techniques of neutralization suggested by Sykes and Matza?
3. What are the differences between denials, excuses, and justifications?
4. Which type of denial do you think is the most serious denial?
5. Why would the various denials, excuses, and justifications be important to corrections professionals?
6. Compare and contrast the consequences of white-collar offenses and conventional offenses.
7. Why is it so easy for offenders to ignore the consequences of their actions?

TABLE 3.5
SOURCE OF DENIAL

Event	*Example*
Financial problem develops	Individual makes risky investment and loses savings that was to be used for child's college tuition, mortgage payments, and boat payments.
Structure problem as nonshareable	Individual is embarrassed about losing the family savings.
Desire for a specific solution is created	The individual dwells on the problem and decides that it needs to be fixed quickly with no one knowing about it.
Exploitation of opportunity	The individual takes advantage of the trust given by the organization and steals to compensate for the losses.
Rationalization	The individual rationalizes his or her actions so that the crime can occur and may continue to commit the crime as a result of the rationalizations.

Source: Adapted from Albanese (1999).

Chapter 4

THE EXPERIENCES OF WHITE-COLLAR INMATES: THE SIX Ds

INTRODUCTION

It is difficult to determine exactly how many white-collar offenders are incarcerated at any given point in time. To be sure, white-collar inmates are in the minority. The question that comes up centers on just how few white-collar inmates there are. At the federal level, estimates about the number of white-collar inmates vary from a low of 0.7 percent (or 1,107) of federal inmates (information obtained from the *Compendium of Federal Justice Statistics*, 2000), to a high of 13 percent (or 20,558) of federal inmates (data adapted from the Bureau of Prisons, 2002). The reason for this range in estimates centers on the differences in white-collar crime definitions. A more narrow definition, such as that followed by the Federal Bureau of Prisons, yields the low estimate, whereas a broader offense-based definition leads to the higher estimates. Still, these higher estimates represent relatively few inmates when the total number of inmates are concerned. As is seen later in this chapter, the fact that they are in the minority leads to an assortment of dilemmas and problems for white-collar inmates, as well as for those who supervise them.

Figure 4.1 provides an estimate of the number of white-collar inmates (defined by the type of offense) in federal prisons in 1999. As shown in the figure, the vast majority of white-collar offenders were accused of fraud, racketeering, or extortion, and a smaller percentage were accused of counterfeiting, embezzlement, and tax law violations. Not all would necessarily agree that these offenses are necessarily always white-collar offenses, but most would agree that those who commit these offenses are often white-collar offenders and that those who commit these kinds of offenses are generally different from those who commit conventional crimes such as robbery, rape, assault, motor vehicle theft, and so on. The estimates provided in Figure 4.1 are not meant to suggest that these figures represent the definitive number of white-collar inmates; rather, they are provided to simply provide an idea about the highest number of white-collar inmates one might to expect in federal prisons at any given time.

FIGURE 4.1. NUMBER OF FEDERAL PRISONERS, BY WHITE-COLLAR OFFENSE, SEPTEMBER 30, 1999.

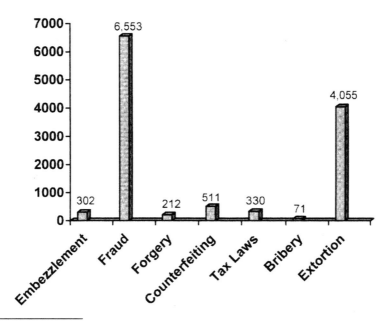

Source: Compendium of Federal Justice Statistics, 1999 (2000), Bureau of Justice Statistics Department of Justice, U.S. Department of Justice. Washington, D.C.: USGPO.

The experiences of white-collar inmates are just as unclear as any estimates about the number of white-collar inmates. The following descriptions describe some experiences of white-collar offenders who spent some time institutionalized for their transgressions:

• Former state trooper David Harding was sentenced to four to nine years in prison after pleading guilty to fabricating fingerprint evidence in four criminal cases, at least one of which was a murder case resulting in the offender receiving a 49 year to life sentence. Given the fact that he was a former police officer and that many offenders "do not take kindly" to police officers, Harding was placed in a special prison unit for his protection. One week he was temporarily moved to another prison so that he could offer testimony in a burglary trial. While being held in the other prison, he was visiting his wife in the visiting room when another inmate walked up to him and said, "You're the reason I'm here." The other inmate, Timothy Vail, then began to beat up Harding, eventually giving him a concussion. This other inmate was, in fact, the offender who received the forty-nine year prison sentence. When he appealed his case on the grounds that Harding's falsified evidence resulted in his wrongful imprisonment, the appellate court ruled that Vail would have been convicted even without the falsified evidence. Still, the fact that Harding and Vail were in a prison visiting room together was "a freakish coincidence" that resulted in harm being brought to Harding (*New York Times*, 1995: B9).

- "Believe it or not, the worst moment was not when I was stabbed and put in solitary confinement-although, if you put splints under my fingernails and told me to tell you what happened in solitary, I couldn't, because the human mind locks these unpleasant thoughts out. No, the worst moment was when I was flown from one prison to another, with my wrists shackled together and a waist chain on, and I had to walk across the airport tarmac with everyone staring at me. And then the two sets of guards from the different prisons argued as to whom the chains belonged to. And I couldn't even go to the bathroom" (Former New York Chief Judge Sol Wachtler told an interviewer this about his 13-month stint in prison, *Psychology Today*, 1997: 30).

- "When I first went into the program, I was, you know, concerned. I didn't know what kind of place I was going to obviously, and I was very concerned about that. I was also concerned about what was going to happen to me, because you hear all these crazy things of what happens in prisons. It upset me to no end. . . . I was a zombie standing around for about two hours and then I went to sleep" (comments from a white-collar offender describing his initial reaction to incarceration, Benson and Cullen, 1988: 209).

The descriptions only begin to capture the full range of emotions experienced by white-collar offenders while incarcerated.

Very little research has considered the experiences of white-collar inmates. Even so, given society's fascination with prison stories and the publicity that comes along with white-collar offenders being sentenced to prison, reports in the media about white-collar offenders' experiences can be combined with the limited amount of research into this area in order to generate understanding about white-collar inmates' experiences. Limited access to these offenders and their offenses by any other method has made it necessary to rely on media accounts to understand the experiences of white-collar inmates.

White-collar crime experts have long recognized the need to use media accounts as a tool to frame our understanding about white-collar crime (Friedrichs, 1996). From the media reports and academic literature on white-collar inmates, six experiences describe the white-collar prisonization experience: (1) depression, (2) danger, (3) deviance, (4) deprivation, (5) denial, and (6) doldrums. The author refers to these experiences as "the six Ds." Table 4.1 shows how each experience surfaces and what these experiences would mean to corrections professionals.

Before discussing these experiences, four points need to be made. First, one should be cognizant of the fact that these experiences are not limited to white-collar inmates. All inmates will, to a degree, experience each of the "six Ds." However, the source of these experiences and their ramifications for corrections professionals vary by type of inmate (e.g., white-collar, conventional). Second, understanding these experiences is useful for corrections professionals because such understanding provides the professionals with the arsenal needed to prevent problems that would arise out of these experiences. Third, the experiences of white-collar inmates will vary from individual to individual, institution to institution, and country to country. For instance, Gerber (1994) reported that in Japan embezzlers are more apt to be treated as street criminals while incarcerated, but in the United States, they are believed to receive less restrictive treatment while imprisoned in the so-called "club fed" institutions. Finally, in discussing these "six Ds," the author uses catchy phrases from songs Elvis Presley sang at one time or another to illustrate what each experience entails. It is important to note that these subheadings are not meant to diminish or make light of the experiences of white-collar inmates. Instead, they are meant to make it easier for the reader to appreciate the experiences in a way that will be simple to remember.

TABLE 4.1
THE SIX DS, WHITE-COLLAR INMATES, AND WHAT THEY MEAN TO CORRECTIONS PROFESSIONALS

Experience	How it is Exhibited	What it Means for Corrections Pofessionals
Depression	Upon incarceration, many inmates may go through stages of shock, grief, and depression.	Because many white-collar inmates enter prison with little prior involvement with the corrections system, they are particularly susceptible to depression. Those who are depressed may act in destructive ways to themselves or others.
Danger	White-collar inmates may be particularly concerned about the dangers they will face while incarcerated.	Regardless of whether the institution is dangerous or not, those who perceive a situation as dangerous may actually become destructive against others as a way to protect themselves.
Deviance	White-collar inmates may engage in various behaviors against prison rules.	Professionals must be careful not to assume that white-collar inmates, many of whom appear very trustworthy, will not engage in illicit actions while they are incarcerated.
Denial	Consistent with the nature of their actions, many white-collar offenders will continue to deny their criminality.	Those in denial will be likely to (1) experience their sanction as too punitive and (2) resist any efforts at rehabilitation.
Deprivation	The nature of imprisonment will cause many white-collar offenders to experience identity changes and an enormous loss of status.	The task for corrections professionals supervising white-collar inmates is to take actions that limit the likelihood that white-collar offenders will leave the institution as a threat to society. Moreover, job placement assistance will be needed by many white-collar inmates.
Doldrums	Many white-collar inmates complain of the boring nature of their confinement.	By limiting boredom, corrections professionals will reduce the likelihood that inmates will engage in destructive behaviors while incarcerated. Many white-collar inmates have skills that can be used to reduce their boredom and help staff and other inmates at the same time.

DEPRESSION–HEARTBREAK HOTEL

At some point during their initial days of incarceration, many white-collar offenders may experience different degrees of depression. To most, who are there for the first time, the entire process is shocking, and it is difficult for white-collar offenders to compare the incarceration experience with "anything they have experienced in their lives" (Breed, 1979: 52). Said one incarcerated white-collar offender of his early days in prison, "For me it was a nightmare" (Pollick, 1998: n.p.). To be certain, depression is something most inmates go through, but it may be more marked for white-collar offenders, particularly because many are incarcerated for the first time (Boothby & Durham, 1999; Douthat, 1989; Marshall, 1993). Three areas are particularly important concerning depression and white-collar inmates: (1) the source of the depression, (2) the warning signs, and (3) the importance of recognizing the symptoms of depression.

Source of Depression in White-Collar Inmates

In addition to the fact that many white-collar offenders have no idea what to expect when they are incarcerated, a number of inter-related factors potentially contribute to depression in white-collar inmates. These factors include stressful changes, separation from family, loss of job or other career obstacles, loss of status, humiliation, disgrace, lack of social support/isolation, and sentencing dynamics.

As far as stressful changes are concerned, it is well established that depression results from negative major life events. Research shows that those that are particularly stressful events are what are called "adverse achievement events" (Mazure et al., 2000). For white-collar inmates, incarceration means that they have failed at the goals they had set for themselves in terms of their family relations and career aspirations. Conventional offenders might expect that they may be sent to jail or prison and, in some circles, incarceration is a status symbol—an achievement in and of itself. This is certainly not the case for white-collar inmates who would experience the incarceration as an adverse achievement event. In the words of a former white-collar inmate, most white-collar offenders "never even dreamed they would end up in jail" (Cutter, 2001: 194).

Separation from family also contributes to depression among inmates. Many white-collar inmates may recognize that their family will go through financial difficulties as a result of their actions. Recognizing their family's suffering, it is common for white-collar inmates to worry that their family will not be there for them when they leave prison (Breed, 1979). Some will also become depressed over the fact that they will not be able to be a part of important family events. For those who do not suffer financially, the lifestyle change of leaving lavish mansions for a sparse prison environment is also a possible source of depression (Wilkie, 1990).

The fact that their incarceration results in the loss of their careers and future aspirations may also lead to depression among some white-collar inmates (Breed, 1979; Fels, 2001; Mazure et al., 2000). In addition to having to worry about financial difficulties for their families, they also will come to find that their lives will center around their crime, or at least the response to their crime, rather than their careers. Former Arizona Governor Fife Symington, who received a two-and-a-half-year prison sentence for defrauding lenders in a bogus development deal, described the change from governor to criminal in the following quote: "The legal avalanche that has resulted from my mistakes has been the most brutal experience in my life" (Nachtigal, 1998: n.p.).

Along a related line, the loss of status, humiliation, and disgrace experienced by white-collar inmates also likely contributes to depression. Most white-collar inmates are individuals who were accustomed to being in charge, but they will certainly not be in charge while incarcerated (Garland, 2000). Consider the following quotes from three different white-collar inmates as an illustration of the way white-collar inmates experience the loss of status, humiliation, and disgrace:

- "You have lost control of your life and that is a really rough thing to get used to" (Cutter, 2001: 196).
- "I feel like I have been asked to swim ten miles up river while hog-tied" (Castillo, 1996: 59).
- "Prison life was a lot different from what I was used to. It was shocking to think that I was now one of them" (Frayler, 2000: 049).

The loss of status in and of itself is felt as a punishment for white-collar offenders (Benson, 1985a). For those who experience incarceration, the loss of status combined with the incarceration experience increases the risk that white-collar inmates, at least initially, will experience some form of depression. These experiences relate directly to the various deprivations experienced by white-collar inmates (discussed later).

Isolation has also been found to increase the possibility of depression, and white-collar offenders, compared to conventional criminals, are certainly an isolated minority. Figures 4.2a, 4.2b, and 4.2c illustrate the percentage of different types of offenders in jails and state and federal prisons. Because figures are not maintained on the actual number of white-collar offenders in jails and prisons, these offense-based definitions would provide a potentially higher estimate of the number of white-collar offenders in the various institutions. In other words, at most, three percent of the inmates in state prisons would be white-collar inmates, five percent of inmates in jails would be white-collar inmates, and 13 percent of the inmates in federal prisons would be white-collar inmates. What this means is that white-collar inmates will be in the minority and will have few peers with whom they can relate while institutionalized (Rokach & Cripps, 1999). One white-collar offender conveyed these feelings in the following description of the prison experience: "It's kind of a rabid state. I don't know anyone else who's in here for a white-collar crime" (Associated Press, 2001b: n.p.).

FIGURE 4.2A. MOST SERIOUS OFFENSE OF FEDERAL INMATES, 1999.

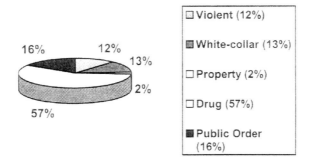

Source: Compendium of Federal Justice Statistics, 1999 (2000), Bureau of Justice Statistics Department of Justice, U.S. Department of Justice. Washington, D.C.: USGPO.

FIGURE 4.2B. MOST SERIOUS OFFENSE OF STATE PRISONERS, 1997.

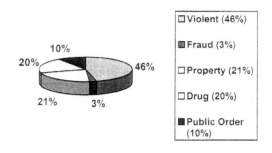

Source: Trends In U.S. Correctional Populations (1998). Bureau of Justice Statistics Department of Justice, U.S. Department of Justice. Washington, D.C.: USGPO.

FIGURE 4.2C. MOST SERIOUS OFFENSE OF JAIL INMATES, 1996.

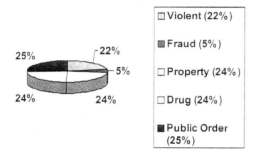

Source: Adapted from Profile of Jail Inmates, 1996. Bureau of Justice Statistics, U.S. Department of Justice, Washington, D.C.: USGPO.

Sentencing dynamics may also contribute to depression in at least three different ways. First, if offenders are sent to an institution far from their family, the difficulty of maintaining family visits may lead to depression among inmates. Second, for those who receive long sentences, frustration may arise when they find that they were sentenced longer than other offenders whom they think are more blameworthy. For instance, a lawyer sentenced to 87 months for federal fraud charges quipped, "I was sentenced to 87 months for buying a bank and [he] got 30 months for robbing one" (Council, 1997: n.p.).

Third, and in stark contrast to the previous point, research shows that those who receive shorter prison sentences may actually have more problems adjusting to prison life than those who receive longer sentences. Those with longer sentences have been found to have "fewer complaints, higher self esteem, and lower anxiety and depression" (Schill & Marcus, 1998: 224). Figure 4.3 outlines the percentage of offenders receiving sentences of less than one year. Nearly half of federal white-collar inmates received a sentence of less than a year, compared to less than one in 12 violent offenders or drug offenders. Given that the vast majority of white-collar offenders receive shorter sentences, they are in a position to have problems getting accustomed to the prison environment, thus increasing the possibility of serving sentences colored by depression. Of course, one would not expect inmates to beg for longer sentences to make it

FIGURE 4.3. PERCENTAGE OF FEDERAL PRISONERS RECEIVING A SENTENCE OF LESS THAN 1 YEAR BETWEEN OCTOBER 1, 1998 AND SEPTEMBER 30, 1999.

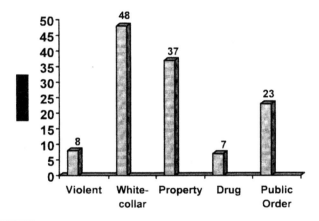

Source: Compendium of Federal Justice Statistics, 1999 (2000). Bureau of Justice Statistics, U.S. Department of Justice, Washington, D.C.: USGPO.

easier to cope.

Warning Signs of Depression

Depression is not limited to white-collar inmates, and not all white-collar inmates will necessarily become depressed. There is, however, a set of warning signs that might indicate that an individual is depressed. A nonexhaustive list of these signs includes the following:

- Diminished interest in activities individuals used to enjoy
- Noticeable weight loss or weight gain not attributable to dieting

- Problems sleeping or sleeping too much
- Feelings of worthlessness
- Feelings of inappropriate guilt
- Physical symptoms, such as headaches or stomachaches
- Suicidal thoughts (Aware Foundation, 2000; Chaudron, 1994).

For white-collar inmates, some of these symptoms may actually be natural responses to the incarceration experience. To adequately assess whether the offender is clinically depressed, it would be necessary to use one of several depression assessment instruments. One simple assessment of depression is offered in the DSM-IV. Specifically, the American Psychiatric Association defines depression in the following manner:

> At least five of the following symptoms are present during the same period; depressed mood or loss of interest or pleasure must be present. Symptoms are present most of the day, nearly daily for almost two weeks:
>
> 1. Depressed mood, most of the day, nearly every day
> 2. Markedly diminished interest or pleasure in almost all activities most of the day, nearly every day (as indicated either by subjective account or observation by others of apathy most of the time)
> 3. Significant weight loss or gain
> 4. Psychomotor agitation or retardation
> 5. Fatigue
> 6. Feelings of worthlessness
> 7. Impaired concentration
> 8. Recurring thoughts of death or suicide.

Recognizing these warning signs of depression can help to effectively manage all inmates, particularly those, such as white-collar inmates, who are at a risk of marked depression.

The Importance of Recognizing Depression

Some may contend that incarceration is not supposed to be easy and that it does not matter if offenders become depressed while they are incarcerated. Such a belief would be shortsighted for a number of reasons. First, depressed white-collar inmates are at a higher risk of suicide (Nash, 1998). Beyond the pure moral duty to prevent individuals from harming themselves, suicides in prisons and jails bring much negative attention from the media, which in itself creates difficulties managing the institutions. Second, depression has been linked to aggressive behaviors against others. Thus, preventing or limiting depression can be a way to reduce violence in institutions (Rokach & Cripps, 1999). Third, inmates who are depressed and never overcome their depression may leave the institution worse off than when they entered. Consequently, the rest of society may pay if the offender reoffends because his or her depression was never handled appropriately.

Fortunately, most white-collar offenders will overcome their initial depression. Indeed, after a period of disorientation, it is believed that many white-collar inmates will see that imprisonment was not as bad as they expected. Those who are most able to deal with the stresses of the prison experience are those who are more educated and those who have strong identities along with a strong commitment to traditional values (Benson & Cullen, 1988). To further reduce the likelihood of depression, some experts recommend that the white-collar defendant's attorney provide the defendant with a general "mock orientation" to prison life. The idea is for the defense attorney to provide the future inmate for "what, most likely, will be one of the worst experiences of his or her life" (Axelrod & Kuca, 1998: n.p.).

DANGER–DON'T BE CRUEL

White-collar inmates may also experience concerns about danger. This is not to suggest that they will be hurt physically, but they will certainly be concerned about their physical well-being, at least initially. Violence, beatings, rapes, and other assaults against white-collar inmates are rare, especially in the federal system (Mize, 2001). But, they do happen. For instance, a former judge was stabbed in the back while he was asleep (McCarthy, 1996). In another case, a white-collar inmate claimed that while incarcerated he had been "robbed of his wedding band by a prisoner with a large knife. . . and extorted by inmates" (Klein, 1996: 1D).

Concerns about sexual assault may be especially heightened during the initial stages of incarceration. However, reports of sexual assault are infrequent, and research suggests that when sexual activity occurs in prisons, it is most often consensual (Saum et al., 1995). What is believed to be common is sexual harassment, especially likely to be targeted toward new inmates. Varieties of sexual harassment in prison include statements feminizing the inmates and sexual propositions (Henderson, 2001; Robertson, 1999).

Although physical assaults and rapes are relatively infrequent against white-collar inmates, they feel especially vulnerable to these assaults for at least six reasons. First, white-collar inmates often believe that these assaults are more common than they actually are. Second, they may be verbally harassed by inmates simply because they make more money, and this harassment results in fear about victimization (Cutter, 2001). Third, some white-collar inmates, especially politicians and those who work in the justice system, are often blamed by the inmates for the inmates' incarceration (Foy, 1995). Fourth, many white-collar inmates feel weaker physically (Pollack & Smith, 1983). Fifth, inmates with longer sentences (more often violent offenders and drug offenders) are not particularly fond of those who receive shorter sentences (Garland, 2000). Finally, some white-collar criminals believe, sometimes justifiably, that they are simply not liked by other offenders. According to a former New York City disc jockey who spent time in a minimum security prison, "Let's just say you're not a welcome addition, and people don't want to be around you" (Saxe, 2000: n.p.).

One of the potential problems that may arise is that individuals who are in fear of danger, even if there is evidence that the fear is irrational, may act in aggressive ways in order to control their fears (Lore, 1992). Here's how one inmate described the "fear influence":

> My fear was so heavy that I kept thinking about it. Day and day and day. And I couldn't get this fear out. I kept trying and I couldn't get it out. I couldn't stand it in jail and so I kept the same bad feelings.... And it wasn't the guard's fault, but one time I jumped him, (Sykes, 1958: 57)

Corrections professionals can use a number of strategies to limit the danger and the perceptions of danger experienced by white-collar inmates, and some would say they have a moral duty to do so (Rackmill, 1992). Regarding fear about sexual assaults, Dallao (1996) suggested a number of strategies to make inmates safer (see Table 4.2). She suggests that staff and inmates should be trained about various issues associated with these assaults, and that procedures should be developed to help intervene should a sexual assault occur. She also noted that inmates should be made aware of things they can do to limit their risks. This would be particularly useful for white-collar inmates. According to one former white-collar inmate, "eighty per-cent of white-collar inmates can avoid violence in prisons. . . . Greed will get you beat up. Fear will get you beat up. You stay out of other people's business" (Henderson, 2001: n.p.). Other strategies that have been shown to reduce victimization risks include better classi-fication, keeping inmates institutionalized close to their families, encouraging family visitation, and increasing involvement in educa-tion and treatment programs (Wooldredge, 1994).

TABLE 4.2
MAKING THE INSTITUTION SAFER

Strategy	Why it is Important
Change staff attitudes	Some corrections professionals are unaware of the nature of sexual assaults in prisons and jails and others tend to believe that the assaults are somehow warrant-ed. Corrections professionals must come to see these assaults in their true light.
Educated offenders	New offenders should be made aware of their risk for assault and be told ways to prevent themselves from falling prey to assaults. For instance, assaults often occur against offenders who are new to the prison environment (which most white-collar offenders are).
Educate staff about preventing sexual assaults	In addition to altering their attitudes, staff must be trained how to prevent sexual assaults.
Educate staff about ways to intervene	Intervening and responding to sexual assaults when they do occur in an institution will limit the likelihood that aggressive inmates will be assaultive in the future.
Inmate orientation	Effective inmate orientation will keep those who are at a high risk of assault from being incarcerated with a more violent population.
Educate the public	The public tends to exaggerate the occurrence of prison rapes making new white-collar inmates particu-larly anxious about their imprisonment. The anxiety could cause some to be destructive to themselves or others

Source: Adapted from Dallao (1996).

DEVIANCE–GOIN' TO A PARTY AT THE COUNTY JAIL

Sociological pioneer Emile Durkheim argued that deviant behavior would exist in all groups of beings—even in a society of saints. If one would expect that deviant behavior would exist among a group of saints, one could certainly conclude that deviant behavior may occur among a group of incarcerated white-collar offenders. Four general types of deviant acts have been committed by white-collar inmates: (1) internal rule violations, (2) external rule violations, (3) deviant use of the justice process, and (4) jailstripe crimes.

Internal rule violations are acts that are prohibited by prison rules, or acts that would be legal in environments other than the institution. Examples of internal rule violations that some white-collar inmates have committed include possession of contraband, gambling, disobeying general prison rules, and consensual sexual activity (Pileggi, 1986; Sciacca, 1997). Many likely recall that Washington D.C. Mayor Marion Barry was accused of engaging in oral sex with a prostitute in the visiting room while he was incarcerated. Allegedly, one of the jail employees was enamored with Barry and arranged the activity (*Daily Telegraph*, 1992). Similar allegations were levied against Air Force officials who supervised white-collar offenders at one federal prison housed on a military base. Specifically, it has been reported that the officials granted "inmates access to a whorehouse near the base in exchange for various favors, including investment counseling" (Bart, 1983: 23).

Administrators must sometimes take sweeping actions to prevent internal rule violations from disrupting institutional routine. For instance, during his fifty-four months in prison, Watergate co-conspirator G. Gordon Liddy organized a food strike with about sixty white-collar offenders at the Allenwood Correctional Facility, a minimum security federal institution near Lewisburg, Pennsylvania. To respond to their ability to organize themselves, federal prison authorities transferred many of the strikers to other institutions (Pileggi, 1986).

External rule violations are actions that would be illegal in any setting. Or, these are crimes that just happen to occur in prison or jail. They may entail the commission of the same or similar offenses for which the inmate is incarcerated. For example, one white-collar inmate continued to rip off his association by using the association's telephone credit card while he was incarcerated (McAllister, 1999). Another white-collar inmate conducted a bank fraud scheme by having his corporate secretary forward calls for hours on end, selling and buying airplanes (*Harper's*, 1999). Still others find new ways to commit occupational offenses. Consider a case where a white-collar offender used a telephone in a prison's busy commons area to get companies' account numbers and subsequently order merchandise charging the defrauded company for thousands of dollars of merchandise which was sent to hotel rooms or mail delivery services (Rolls, 1998). In a separate case, a white-collar inmate defrauded women he met through "lonely hearts" advertisements by promising to give the women access to his money (*Harper's*, 1999).

Deviant use of the justice process occurs when white-collar offenders misuse the justice process, generally done in an attempt to avoid punishment. Excessive and inappropriate use of civil litigation, inappropriately changing parole dates, and misuse of prison treatment programs are examples of deviant use of the justice process. It is common to hear about the plethora or prisoner lawsuits, and though no research has considered whether white-collar inmates are overrepresented in these cases, there is no reason to believe that they do not file their fair share of lawsuits. Regarding altering parole dates, though uncommon, one white-collar offender successfully applied for parole although his plan agreement with the court stipulated, "under no circumstances shall the defendant be eligible for shock probation or parole" (Ewinger, 1995: 1B).

Misuse of prison treatment programs occurs when white-collar inmates inappropriately gain access into a program in order to earn good time credits or some other form of early release. For example, the Bureau of Prison's Residential Drug Abuse Treatment Program is available for federal drug offenders who are willing to receive five-hundred hours of drug treatment, counseling, education, and group therapy. Those who complete the program will have their sentence reduced up to one year. Some white-collar offenders are believed to apply for the program not because they have a drug problem, but because they want a sentence reduction. Said one law enforcement official, "It's amazing how it seems every fraud on Wall Street says they abuse drugs. But maybe every fraud on Wall Street does abuse drugs" (Barrett, 2001: 24). Federal officials say that strict psychological screening tests keep out most offenders who truly have no drug problem.

Jailstripe crimes are occupational offenses committed while working on some prison job or duty. Prison chaplain George Castillo
(1996) shared the story of a former banker who literally begged to be
appointed chairperson of the prison's fundraising committee. As
chairperson, the banker nearly doubled the amount of funds raised
from $5,500 to $9,100 in a one-year time frame. Reverend Castillo
eventually learned that the former banker had promised the inmates
he'd put in a good word for them to get them an early release date if
they made the maximum contribution. Later, he prepared a letter
for the chaplain to sign stating that the inmates' efforts should be
rewarded with extra time in the halfway house. As you might expect,
Castillo never signed the letter.

Many of these deviant acts likely occur because white-collar
inmates are afforded a level of trust. Arguing that corrections professionals must not fall into the trap a misplacing their trust in inmates,
Bayse (1995: 68) wrote the following:

> Inmates have lots of time on their hands, and they are constantly watching
> for employees who they feel would be susceptible to manipulation. They
> listen to conversations and watch constantly to find a "duck" to target.
> Most likely candidates are employees who are discontented with the job,
> having marital or financial problems, under stress, or experiencing any-
> thing else the inmates perceive as weaknesses. Then . . . they use this
> information to play a deadly "game" designed to fulfill their desires for
> drugs, sex, goods, services, and most of all—power.

Gladwin (1999) adds that corrections professionals should not toler-
ate the following actions:

- Discussions of one's personal life (especially sex) with inmates.
- Relaxing rules or allowing special treatment for some inmates.
- Allowing inmates to do favors for staff.
- Talking to inmates about other inmates or staff.

Though neither Gladwin nor Bayse specifically cited white-collar
inmates, the fact that most criminal justice professionals can relate to
the plight of white-collar offenders implies that professionals might
be inclined to trust white-collar inmates more than conventional
inmates. Out of fear of being transferred to a more severe prison

environment, most white-collar inmates will not commit deviant acts while incarcerated. Those who do, however, will create major headaches for staff and administrators. Consequently, corrections professionals must be cautious not to place too much trust in the inmates.

DEPRIVATIONS–YOU'VE LOST THAT LOVIN' FEELING

Like other inmates, white-collar inmates will experience certain deprivations and these deprivations certainly relate to the experience of depression considered earlier. The deprivations experienced by white-collar inmates, however, are distinct in many ways from those deprivations experienced by conventional inmates. White-collar criminals may experience any of five related deprivations: 1) loss of status, 2) loss of privacy, 3) identity loss, 4) loss of freedom, and 5) loss of future. These deprivations and the way they are manifested among white-collar inmates are addressed in Table 4.3.

TABLE 4.3
DEPRIVATIONS EXPERIENCED BY WHITE-COLLAR INMATES

Source	How White-Collar Offenders Experience This
Loss of status	Referred to as a fall from grace, the white-collar inmates status changes more than conventional inmates because they fall further down the "social class ladder."
Lack of privacy	White-collar inmates, like other inmates, have virtually no privacy. Unlike conventional inmates, they have fewer peers with whom they can identify while they are incarcerated.
Identity loss	Many white-collar inmates will lose their sense of self when they are incarcerated. Because they served time, white-collar inmates will be labeled negatively by members of society. In their peer group criminal justice involvement is seen as a blight in ones character. For many conventional criminals, criminal justice involvement is seen as a sign of status among their peers.
Loss of freedom	Like conventional inmates, white-collar offenders lose their freedom. The loss of freedom experienced by white-collar inmates, particularly those who had no previous involvement with the justice system, was more unexpected and potentially more difficult to accept.
Loss of future	Because they committed crimes related to their career, their future as they once imagined it ceased to exist. Most will never be able to work in their original career.

Loss of Status

Loss of status was briefly considered as a source of depression, but it can also be seen as a deprivation experienced by many white-collar inmates. Recall that incarceration may be seen as a status symbol for some conventional criminals, but this is certainly not the case with white-collar offenders. To put this into perspective, Ivan Boesky went from turning his mother-in-law's $700,000 estate into a $200 million profit to making eleven cents an hour working as a janitor at a federal prison camp after being convicted for his part in the savings and loan fiasco (Hall, 1989). Describing this loss of status, one white-collar inmate said, "imagine how devastating it is. I took off a pair of Calvin Klein underwear and put on my prison boxer shorts" (Pollick, 1998: n.p.).

The loss of status is something that continues to follow white-collar offenders once they leave the institution. As Weisburd and Waring (2001: 921) told us, "Because imprisonment is unlikely to be a common experience in the lives of friends and family of white-collar offenders, the stigmatization associated with prison may be greater for white-collar offenders." In the words of a former white-collar inmate: "So here I am—free but a felon. Bad jobs. Can't vote. I lost my house, animals, credit cards, and a lot of my friends. And I lost the opportunity to give my children what I never had" (Frayler, 2000: 04A).

Loss of Privacy

White-collar inmates also experience *loss of privacy.* To be sure, all inmates will experience privacy losses, but there may be more of a loss for white-collar inmates. For instance, white-collar inmates have fewer peers with whom they can identify. Consequently, their privacy is lost to a larger group of "strangers," while the privacy loss experienced by conventional criminals is lost to a group with whom the conventional criminals can identify. Moreover, it is believed that there is more of a privacy loss in federal institutions, where many white-collar inmates are housed, simply because of the barracks style housing found in many of the institutions. According to one federal white-collar inmate, "We have communal bathrooms, barracks-style bedrooms, and virtually no time alone" (Andresky, 1984: 135). A rather optimistic white-collar inmate found some benefits to this type of living when he stated, "Rarely, if ever, will you have to sit on a cold toilet seat" (Marshall, 1993: 21).

Identity Loss

White-collar inmates will also undergo an *identity loss* while incarcerated. Loss of identity has been described by some offenders as the worst aspect of incarceration. Essentially they find themselves changing from respected citizen to prisoner (Loane, 2000). A former celebrated baseball player who served time for his misdeeds said, "When you walk through that gate, you're no longer [yourself]. I was just another inmate with a number" (Wilkie, 1990: A1). Trying to describe this identity loss, Watergate coconspirator John Ehrlichman wrote the following to inside trader Ivan Boesky prior to Boesky's prison sentence:

> You are about to enter a bizarre micro-culture so different from your life as a wealthy father, husband, lawyer, and Wall Street titan that you will feel that you have dropped into a totally foreign society. As you look around, you will notice that there are no children or dogs or cats. It is a society where the audience cheers the bad guys in the movies. (Knox, 1999: n.p.)

This process of identity change was particularly noted in the classic Stanford Prison Experiment. Testifying before Congress about his well-known prison experiment, Zimbardo (1971) stated:

> At the end of only six days we had to close down our mock prison because what we saw was frightening. It was no longer apparent to us or most of the subjects where they ended and their roles began. The majority had indeed become "prisoners" or "guards," no longer able to clearly differentiate between role-playing and self. There were dramatic changes in virtually every aspect of their behavior, thinking and feeling. In less than a week, the experience of imprisonment undid (temporarily) a lifetime of learning; human values were suspended, self-concepts were challenged . . . the ugliest, most base, pathological side of human nature surfaced. We were horrified because we saw some boys ("guards") treat other boys as if they were despicable animals, taking pleasure in cruelty, while other boys ("prisoners") became servile, dehumanized robots who thought only of escape, of their own individual survival, and of their mounting hatred of the guards.

Simply being in a mock institution changed the identities of the students. One might conclude a similar process may occur among some white-collar inmates.

The process of identity loss is important for corrections professionals for at least four overlapping reasons. First, those who experience identity loss may be prone to engage in unexpected behaviors (e.g., violence, rule infractions, etc.). Corrections professionals should watch for any signs of these behaviors.

Second, identity loss could trigger a reaction to the incarceration in that the offender will become more hardened rather than rehabilitated. Said one white-collar inmate: "Prison is no more than graduate crime school. We virtually guarantee they'll come out worse than when they went in" (Sachs, 1989, cited in Balsmeier & Kelly, 1996: 145). One author described how this graduate crime school operated:

> After dinner, many of the men adjourn to "seminars" where experts in various fields of criminality exchange their knowledge in laundering money, breaking computer codes, and swindling insurance companies. [The prison] after dark becomes a kind of Harvard Business School, where men who have controlled the megabucks of Big Business can meet with men who controlled the megabucks of Big Drugs to find new ways of enriching one another. (Bart, 1983: 23)

It is important to note that many white-collar inmates choose not to enroll in this "graduate crime school" and instead prefer to be isolated so that they can maintain their preoffense identities (Benson & Cullen, 1988). One might say that they are doing "independent studies."

Third, corrections professionals must keep in mind that white-collar inmates will experience the identity loss in different ways. For some, the identity loss will be negative. For others, the identity loss may actually serve to help the offender cope with imprisonment. Former Arizona Governor and subsequent white-collar convict Fife Symington offered this advice to future white-collar inmates: "First, he has to forget himself. He has got to forget about who he was in the outside world. If he doesn't acknowledge that, if he doesn't forget that, he'll do hard time. The best thing he can do is forget who he is" (Flannery, 1998: A7).

Finally, and on a related point, note that in some cases the identity loss may actually serve a beneficial function in that some offenders will change themselves into individuals with whom they are more satisfied. This process of transformation will be discussed in more detail in the next chapter. For now, it is sufficient to suggest that incarceration has been known to actually do wonders for some white-collar inmates, and corrections professionals could manipulate the incarceration process to ensure that it is beneficial rather than detrimental to the identity change experienced by the white-collar inmate.

Loss of Freedom

Another deprivation white-collar inmates will experience is the loss of freedom. Because these are individuals who are used to being in charge, the loss of freedom may be a particularly difficult adjustment for some white-collar inmates. In the words of one white-collar inmate, "It's hard to always be told what to do" (Andresky, 1984: 114). A prison official echoed this sentiment stating, "The greatest thing an individual can lose is his freedom" (Bacon, 1988). For white-collar inmates, some assume that the freedom loss is minimal because they are generally in minimum security institutions. Most white-collar inmates would express contempt for an assumption such as this one. As a former swindler said, "When a man has lost his freedom, he could be locked up in the fanciest hotel in Dallas and he'd still be a prisoner" (Gest, 1985: 43). The following quote from a federal prison warden echoes this inmate's sentiment: "You can walk out of a country club whenever you want to, but you can't walk out of here whenever you want" (Waga, 1991: n.p.). The key for corrections professionals in regard to loss of freedom is to help to educate the public and the media so that all parties can see that all inmates truly lose their freedom. Ways to alert the public about the punitive nature of minimum security prisons, and related freedom losses, are considered in the next chapter.

Loss of Future

Some white-collar inmates will also experience what can be called a *loss of future* when they are incarcerated. Alluded to in the previous section on depression, this deprivation entails the fact that white-col-

lar inmates will need to change their career aspirations and goals.
An attorney serving time went from making $766,000 a year to mak-
ing 41 cents an hour working a photocopier. He said, "When I had
my law practice, I had ten assistants who did my paperwork. That
stopped cold, along with the income" (Goldman, 2001: 204). This
attorney is not alone in losing a career. A study of legal violations by
Alabama lawyers over an eight-year time frame found that nearly
three-fourths attorneys convicted of a felony (14 of 19) either lost
their licenses or were disbarred (Payne and Stevens, 1999).

Attorneys are not alone in their loss of future; indeed, most white-
collar inmates will have to change their career paths. Although the
loss of future seems like it would always negative, given the right
kind of guidance from corrections professionals, as will be shown in
the next chapter, the new future of white-collar inmates does not
have to be bleak.

DENIAL–YOUR CHEATIN' HEART

It should not be surprising that the experience of denial, considered in the previous chapter, is part of the prison experience for
some white-collar offenders. Seeing that they are virtually alone in
their incarceration, many white-collar offenders want to know why
they were singled out for a jail or prison sentence (Bart, 1983). It is
likely that imprisonment will not deter future misconduct of those
who continue to deny their criminality throughout their incarceration. One offender in denial made the following comments: "At least
I'm putting the time to good use. I've been studying everything I can
get my hands on–Spanish, auditing, tax shelters, counterfeiting. If
the fucking cops want to call me a crook, at least I'll be a versatile
crook" (Bart, 1983: 26).

After the initial shock of incarceration, some white-collar offenders will begin a process of reconciliation and may begin to see how
they were responsible for their misconduct (Benson & Cullen, 1988).
There are various degrees of remorse that will surface in this reconciliation process (see Figure 4.4). Some offenders feel remorse about
getting caught, others feel remorse about getting punished, others
feel remorse for hurting their family, and others feel remorse for
their actions. Some white-collar inmates may show remorse only as

a means of re-establishing trust, allowing them to continue in their misconduct. One white-collar offender pleaded with the court, "All I want to say is, I am sorry for the damage that has been done. I didn't intentionally do it. It didn't work out the way I planned" (Klein, 1996: 1D). Later the same day, the offender cashed a bogus $40,000 check. The next day he changed a check from his wife's account from $200 to $200,000. After serving a seven-and-a-half- year prison sentence for these offenses, and again showing remorse, he returned to the same white-collar crime lifestyle. The type of remorse would seem to relate to the highest likelihood of reoffending.

FIGURE 4.4. REMORSE EXTREMES AMONG WHITE-COLLAR INMATES.

Remorse for getting caught	Remorsefor getting punished	Remorse for harm to family	Remorse for committing the crime
High likelihood of reoffending	Moderate likelihood of reoffending	Lower likelihood of reoffending	Lowest likelihood of reoffending

Source: Adapted from Nash (1998)

Although examples of false remorse have been illustrated here, many white-collar inmates overcome their denial and return to a crime-free lifestyle. The point for corrections professionals to remember is that words of remorse are simply that—words. Actions speak louder than words, and professionals should not assume that apologies are always heartfelt.

DOLDRUMS–I'M SO LONELY I COULD CRY

Once white-collar inmates see that prison is not as dangerous as they thought, and that it is not as horrible as they expected, the other major obstacle they report facing is a huge case of the doldrums. They are just plain bored. Some white-collar offenders claim that time seems to move slower in minimum security prisons (Breed, 1979). In fact, boredom and monotony have been cited as the worst part of the white-collar inmate's incarceration experiences (Coughlin, 1994; Goldman, 2001). One former white-collar inmate who spent eighteen months in a federal prison to those facing similar stints advised: "Your greatest obstacle will be the time itself. There will be days that seem to last forever. You can do 'hard time' or 'easy time'— it all depends on your attitude and approach" (TerMeer, 1997: 20). A task for corrections professionals is to find ways to make inmates' experiences "easy time" because this would increase the efficiency of the administration of the institution. Decreasing boredom through various programs could actually make time easier and reduce the likelihood that white-collar inmates will engage in deviant actions while incarcerated. As the adage goes, "the idle mind is the devil's workshop."

CONCLUDING REMARKS

White-collar inmates will certainly experience a range of emotions while imprisoned. Although the "six Ds" have been discussed separately, they are often experienced simultaneously. Kubler-Ross's (1970) description of the stages of grieving offers just one way to illustrate how various emotions may result from an unwanted experience (See Table 4.4).

First, when individuals have something happen to them (such as incarceration), they will go through a stage of denial trying to make themselves believe that there has been some sort of mistake. Next, individuals will become angry about the unwanted event. For corrections professionals, it is important to realize that anger may trigger aggressive acts by inmates. Third, individuals will offer various bargains to get out of their unwanted situation. For instance, white-collar offenders may search for legal loopholes or strategies to reduce their sentence. Fourth, when individuals realize that the unwanted situation cannot be changed, they may become depressed. Recall that depression may lead to violent actions. Finally, at some point most individuals will come to terms with the unwanted event through the process of acceptance. In fact, most white-collar offenders come to grips with the fact that they have to serve their time. According to one state prison warden, "[white-collar criminals] are survivors in a sense. They're intelligent people, and they're able to adjust. Many of them actually find it very intriguing" (Lore, 1992: 1F).

TABLE 4.4
SOURCE OF DENIAL

Stage	Implications
Denial	Those in denial will have difficulty understanding why they are incarcerated and will be resistant to any sort of treatment
Anger	Those who are angry will be at a higher risk of hurting themselves or others.
Bargaining	Many white-collar inmates will seek legal loopholes or strategies to reduce their sentence.
Depression	Depressed white-collar inmates are at a higher risk of hurting themselves or others.
Acceptance	At some point, most white-collar inmates will accept their sanction and will abide by the rules of the institution simply because they are afraid of being transferred to a more difficult prison environment.

Once they have accepted their prison sentence, white-collar offenders will utilize various strategies to cope in prison. Benson & Cullen (1988) cited three common coping strategies. First, some white-collar offenders will continue with elitist attitudes in order to maintain their high self-esteems while they are incarcerated. Second, some white-collar inmates will bond with similar white-collar inmates in order to reduce their isolation, give themselves perspective about their situation, and distance themselves from conventional inmates. Third, most white-collar inmates will conform with the rules as a way to cope with the prison experience. They come to terms with the fact that if they do what is expected of them, they can remain in a lower security prison. If they violate the rules, they realize their situation can become significantly worse.

Based on the way white-collar offenders experience incarceration, a number of strategies can be suggested to effectively supervise and treat them. These strategies are considered in the next chapter.

APPLIED CRITICAL THINKING QUESTIONS

1. Why would white-collar inmates be susceptible to depression?
2. How could concerns about danger influence the actions of white-collar inmates?
3. What kinds of rule infractions might we expect white-collar inmates to commit in prison?
4. How is the dehumanization of white-collar inmates different from the dehumanization of conventional inmates?
5. What can be done to decrease the boredom of confinement for inmates?
6. Should white-collar inmates receive different treatment from corrections officials than what is received by conventional inmates? Explain
7. How would the stages of grief relate to incarceration?

Chapter 5

SUPERVISING AND TREATING WHITE-COLLAR OFFENDERS IN INSTITUTIONS AND THE COMMUNITY: RESTORING THE PUBLIC GOOD

INTRODUCTION

White-collar offenders who are punished by the justice system, whether by incarceration or some other sanction, will have different needs and different things to offer to the punishment experience than other offenders. Consider the following illustrations:

- A relatively unknown lawyer and appellate judge from Houston, Texas, had his seventy-seven day-career as a judge interrupted by a perjury conviction and a subsequent prison sentence. Because he was relatively unknown, classification specialists determined it would be appropriate to place the former judge with the general population at Huntsville prison. Eventually, one of the corrections officials learned that the judge was "a marked man." He was placed in solitary confinement where a routine search uncovered evidence that someone had carefully planted lighter fluid in the light socket in the ex-judge's cell. Soon thereafter, the judge was transferred to federal custody (Castlebury, 2001).

- One afternoon, a well dressed man spoke to a group of disadvantaged teens asking them how many of them would want to trade places with him. Seeing the man, whom they knew as a real estate attorney, so impeccably dressed, all of the teens raised their hands. The man then explained to the youth that he was a former real estate attorney who was completing a prison sentence for defrauding his clients. Suddenly, none of the teens wanted to trade places with the well-dressed speaker. They had learned that white-collar crime can result in negative consequences just like other crimes (Miller, 1996).

- Many institutions, federal prisons in particular, house a number of different kinds of white-collar offenders. Inmates often informally look to those from various occupations for different sorts of advice. In one case, inmates from a federal prison in Pennsylvania wrote letters to a surgeon, on trial for fraudulent activities, asking the surgeon to consider coming to their prison because there were no surgeons serving in their population (Swanson, 2001).

These illustrations suggest that white-collar offenders may need special considerations during different phases of their punishment and that they can be used in ways that benefit themselves and the community. At this point, it is logical to further address the reasons why we incarcerate white-collar offenders and to suggest strategies to effectively respond to white-collar offenses in ways that would be the most beneficial to victims and the community. Also note that white-collar inmates will eventually return to the community and that many white-collar offenders receive community-based sanctions to begin with. Thus, a review of the various community-based sanctions given to white-collar offenders is also warranted. Based on the experiences of white-collar offenders in the corrections process, this chapter will conclude with a number of tips for corrections professionals who are supervising or treating white-collar offenders, whether they are institutionalized or sentenced to a community-based sanction.

WHY PUNISH WHITE-COLLAR OFFENDERS?

Criminologists cite five related reasons why offenders should be punished: 1) to treat the offender, 2) to separate the offender from society, 3) to punish the offender, 4) to deter future misconduct, and 5) to restore the victim and the community to their normal states. These reasons cut across all types of crimes, but the ability of punishment to fulfill each of these reasons varies between type of crime (e.g., white-collar, conventional crime) and type of punishment (incarceration versus community-based sanctions).

As far as rehabilitation is concerned, the idea is that correctional intervention can help to fix whatever caused the individual to commit the crime. In terms of white-collar offenders, however, many argue that they are not in need of treatment simply because they are not like conventional criminals. The majority do not have drug problems, do not associate with other criminals, or partake in other activities seen as the cause of conventional crime. White-collar inmates will need different forms of treatment, however, if for no other reason than to help them cope with their loss of status (Benson, 1985b).

Some also argue that offenders should be incarcerated in order to separate them from society, thereby protecting society. Known as the incapacitation punishment justification, this punishment function applies more to conventional criminals than to white-collar criminals insofar as incarceration is concerned. Incarcerating robbers, burglars, rapists, and others is justified in that these offenders would not be able to commit criminal acts while imprisoned. To be sure, white-collar offenders who are incarcerated are limited in their abilities to commit crime. The issue that comes up is that there are less restrictive alternatives that would keep white-collar offenders from committing future offenses. For instance, if doctors, lawyers, politicians, or accountants lost their licenses or careers, then their likelihood of offending in those careers is virtually eliminated. So, why would we incarcerate white-collar offenders? Some argue that incarceration punishes offenders and is an effective deterrent to future misconduct.

As far as punishment is concerned, from a retributive orientation, it is believed that offenders deserve to be punished. Combining the retributive orientation with deterrence theory, many argue that imprisonment deters future white-collar misconduct (Fels, 2001). A great deal of public support for the deterrent potential of incarcerating white-collar offenders exists, despite the fact that there is very little empirical evidence to support the deterrent potential of incarceration for this group of offenders. Research by Weisburd et al. (1995: 587) on 743 white-collar offenders found that prison "does not have a specific deterrent impact on the likelihood of re-arrest over a 126 month period after release." Earlier research by Weisburd and his associates (1993) found that nearly half of one-thousand white-collar offenders reoffended after their release. Those who are believed to be most likely to re-offend are white-collar offenders with several prior convictions (Soothill et al., 1997) and middle-class white-collar offenders (Weisburd & Waring, 2001).

The logical question to ask is why imprisonment does not deter white-collar misconduct. There are two plausible answers to this question. First, some suggest that although white-collar criminals are believed to be among the more rational criminals, "those who commit these crimes do not completely realize how much is at risk" (Balsmeier & Kelly, 1996: 143). This implies that the general deterrent power of imprisonment is minimal because offenders are not aware of the fact that they could actually be sent to jail for their misdeeds. Second, some, like famed attorney Allan Dershowitz, argue that the sentencing of white-collar offenders is so random that the result is seen as "roulette justice" or "the luck of the draw" (Cohen, 1990: A1). Recall from Chapter 2 that deterrence theory is based on the assumption that punishment must be swift, severe enough to outweigh the pleasure one receives from the act, and certain. The uncertainty of the sanction is seen as minimizing the deterrent potential of incarceration.

Despite evidence that incarceration does not deter misconduct, a number of individuals still make claims about the deterrent aspect of incarcerating white-collar offenders. In the words of Stanford law professor and former SEC Commissioner Joseph Grundfest, "More executives should be going to jail. That will grab their attention . . . and hand a valuable lesson to their entire economy" (Holding & Carlsen, 1999: A1). Some white-collar inmates also see the deterrent aspect of their sanction. As an illustration, one said, "It's hard to accept the fact that you can no longer come and go as you please. But listen. This is prison. It's not supposed to be fun. It's supposed to teach you a lesson" (Cutter, 2001:196).

In response to evidence that current punishment strategies are not working to deal with the crime problem, restorative justice ideals, a rapidly emerging framework for changing the way society views criminals and responds to crime, has been the subject of a great deal of attention in the 1980s and 1990s. The specific ideals of restorative justice are outlined in Table 5.1. Led by criminologists Gordon Bazemore and Mark Umbriet, advocates of restorative justice ideals suggest that crime should be broadened in both conception and response. Crime is not simply an illegal act, but it is an act that brings harm to victims and the community. Consequently, victims and the community should be involved in the response to crime. It is easy to see how white-collar crime is an offense that harms victims and the community. Changing the response to white-collar crime to a restorative justice framework requires a different set of goals in handling white-collar offenders.

TABLE 5.1

GUIDING PRINCIPLES/VALUES OF RESTORATIVE JUSTICE

(Created for the National Institute of Corrections Nationwide Videoconference held December 12, 1996.)

1. Crime is an offense against human relationships.
2. Victims and the community are central to justice processes.
3. The first priority of justice processes is to assist victims.
4. The second priority is to restore the community, to the degree possible.
5. The offender has personal responsibility to victims and to the community for crimes committed.
6. Stakeholders share responsibilities for restorative justice through partnerships for action.
7. The offender will develop improved competency and understanding as a result of the restorative justice experience.

Source: National Institute of Justice.

Table 5.2 lists the differences between restorative justice ideals and retributive justice ideals. Three elements define the way a restorative justice framework would respond to white-collar offending: accountability, community protection, and competency development (Bazemore & Umbriet, 1994). *Accountability* refers to taking actions to ensure that the offender accepts responsibility and makes amends for his or her harmful actions. Accountability is achieved through strategies such as restitution and community service. *Community protection* entails strategies that would ensure that offenders are engaged in fruitful activities that would limit their time, and their desire, for criminal activity. *Competency development* entails giving offenders the experience they would need to succeed in the society (Bazemore & Umbriet, 1994). Given that most convicted white-collar offenders will lose their jobs, they may need assistance, or at the very least direction, in developing competence for a new career.

TABLE 5.2
RETRIBUTIVE JUSTICE VERSUS RESTORATIVE JUSTICE

	Retributive Justice	*Restorative Justice*
Definition of crime	Crime is an act committed against the state or a law violation.	Crime is a harmful act against a person or community.
Crime control source	Criminal justice system	Community
Definition of accountability	Punishing the offender	Assuming responsibility and repairing harm
Punishment ideology	Punishment deters crime	Punishment is not enough in and of itself, may do more harm than good
Victim role	Peripheral	Central role
Temporal focus	On offender's past behavior to justify punishment	On current problem solving strategies and future obligations
Victim/offender/community relationship	Adversarial	Dialog and negotiation
Resolution method	Inflict pain to deter crime	Restitution to restore parties
Community role	Peripheral	Central

Source: Adapted from Bazemore, G. & M. Umbriet (1994).

Restorative justice ideals are more often applied to community-based sanctions, but they can also be applied in jails and prisons. In institutions, restorative justice ideals would strive to:

- Develop offender awareness of injury to victims.
- Involve offenders in repairing the harm.
- Involve the community in the process of holding the offender accountable.
- Increase offender competence.
- Increase the offender's connection to conventional community members (Roerich, 1998:373).

Suffering a staggering loss of status, white-collar offenders may need special attention in order to reconnect them with the conventional community.

A basic assumption of restorative justice ideals is that victims should have multiple choices, and their needs should be central to the response to the crime (Bazemore & Pranis, 1997; Bazemore & Schiff, 2001). This notion is particularly applicable to white-collar crime victims in that there is variation in what white-collar crime victims want from the justice system. Some victims would rather get their money back, but there is very little chance of this occurring when white-collar offenders are sent to prison (Posner, 1980; Roberts, 2000). For those who want their money back, fines, restitution, and community service are seen as appropriate responses. Other victims realize that the offender has likely squandered the stolen money and that their chances of being repaid are minimal. In these cases, victims support long prison sentences (Galvin, 2000). Victims who want their money back are more likely to recover their losses when the offender is living in the community, whether as a parolee or a probationer.

COMMUNITY-BASED SANCTIONS AND WHITE-COLLAR OFFENDERS

Most convicted white-collar offenders will receive some form of community-based sanction. Even though many federal white-collar offenders receive a short prison stint, on release from prison they usually receive some form of community supervision. The importance of understanding community-based alternatives as they relate to white-collar offenders is especially important in the context of a restorative justice framework.

Figure 5.1 shows the number of white-collar offenders, as compared to other types of offenders, who received some form of community supervision as a result of a federal conviction between 1992 and 1996. This figure includes inmates sentenced directly to a community-based alternative and those who received the community-based sanction after incarceration. The number of white-collar offenders under some type of community supervision remained relatively stable throughout this timeframe, and they actually represent a significant proportion of those inmates under community supervision, with nearly one-fourth of federal offenders supervised in the community being white-collar offenders.

A smaller proportion of offenders receiving community supervision at the state and local levels are white-collar offenders. Table 5.3

FIGURE 5.1. TRENDS IN COMMUNITY SUPERVISION POPULATION OF
FEDERAL OFFENDERS, BY TYPE OF OFFENSE COMMITTED,
FISCAL YEARS, 1992–1996

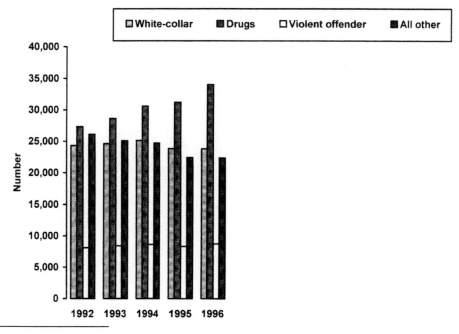

Source: Adapted from *Trends in Community Supervision of Federal Offenders* (1997).

outlines the most serious offenses of adult offenders on probation in
1995. If fraud is used as an indicator of white-collar crime, then just
7 percent of adult probationers are white-collar offenders. Recall
from the previous chapter that everyone who commits fraud is not
necessarily a white-collar offender, meaning that this would be the
highest percentage of white-collar probationers we would expect at
the state and local levels. The fact that there are so few white-collar
probationers making up the caseload of state and local probation
and parole officers has important implications for the supervision of
these offenders. Primarily, many officers may not be trained or capable of supervising a "different breed" of offender. Says white-collar
crime expert Michael Benson (1985b: 435): "officers may be ill
equipped to supervise their social equals or betters."

Indeed, if the traditional goals of the justice process are followed,
probation and parole officers have very little to offer white-collar
offenders, most of whom really do not need the typical services
offered by probation and parole officers (Benson, 1982, 1985).

TABLE 5.3
MOST SERIOUS OFFENSES BY PROBATIONERS IN STATE COURTS, 1995

| *Most* | *Severity of Offense/a* | | |
Serious Offense	*Total/b*	*Felony*	*Misdemeanor*
Violent offenses	17.3	19.5	13.5
Homicide	0.7	1.0	0.2
Sexual assault	3.6	5.6	0.4
Robbery	1.9	3.2	0
Assault	9.2	7.6	11.1
Other Violent	2.0	2.1	1.7
Property offenses	.28.9	36.6	18.2
Burglary	5.8	9.7	0.3
Larceny/theft	9.9	11.1	8.5
Motor vehicle theft	1.4	2.0	0.4
Fraud	7.2	9.6	4.2
Stolen property	1.7	2.3	0.9
Other property	2.7	1.9	3.8
Drug offenses	21.4	30.7	7.6
Possession	9.8	13.1	4.6
Trafficking	9.7	15.4	1.6
Other/unspecified drug	1.9	2.3	1.4
Public order offenses	31.1	12.1	59.6
Weapons	2.3	2.5	2.1
Obstruction of justice	2.2	1.3	3.3
Traffic	4.7	0.9	10.2
Driving while intoxicated	16.7	5.2	35.2
Drunkenness/morals	2.1	0.5	4.5
Other	3.0	1.7	4.3
Other	1.3	1.0	1.2
Number of probationers	2,595,499	1,479,904	988,033

Source: Bonczar, T. P. (1997).

Remember that most do not have drug problems, will stay away from the criminal element, and will have strong work ethics. Consequently, probation and parole officers will not have to focus strongly on keeping white-collar offenders away from drugs or other offenders, and they will not have to help them develop a work ethic. If one were focusing on restorative justice ideals, however, then probation and parole officers would want to encourage offenders to become accountable for their actions and make amends with their victims for their misdeeds.

Moreover, given that most white-collar offenders supervised in the community pose a minimal risk of engaging in other offenses, one of the most important roles of probation and parole officers who supervise white-collar offenders is to help offenders to adjust to their status as a convicted offender (Benson, 1985b). Benson (1985b: 432) quoted one probation officer who described his experiences with one white-collar probationer:

> I've tried to help him deal more effectively with the intense anger he feels at the prosecutor and the judge in this case. I think he needlessly works himself up into a rage over it and I've been trying to help him deal with the fact that the only person he is hurting when he does this is himself. The only thing he did with me is to ventilate some feelings about the prosecution and the conviction.

If offenders are having problems accepting their status as a convicted offender, they will be less prone to become accountable, making restorative justice ideals difficult to meet. Those focusing on restorative justice ideals will need to help offenders cope with their loss of status. This may also include helping them to find employment so they are able to pay restitution to the victims. For those who are employed, one author team implies that their hard work ethic will lead white-collar offenders to adhere to the conditions of probation and parole (paying fees, community service, and so on) in a business-like fashion (Smith & Berlin, 1981). With all probationers and parolees, a number of conditions may be part of the community-based sanction, though the utility of some of these conditions may vary between conventional criminals and white-collar criminals. Also, some conditions are more likely than others to meet restorative justice ideals.

Community Supervision Conditions and White-Collar Offenders

When sentenced to probation or released from prison on parole, most offenders are expected to adhere to certain conditions as established in their sentence. The most common condition given to federal offenders is mandatory drug or substance abuse treatment followed by community service, mental health treatment, and home confinement. Figure 5.2 shows the trends regarding the frequency of each condition between 1992 and 1996. Drug abuse treatment, home confinement, and mental health treatment conditions increased slightly while there was a slight decrease in the condition of community service (*Trends in Community Supervision of Offenders*, 1997). Table 5.4 shows that conditions given to state and local probationers. Common conditions for these probationers include fines, restitution, substance abuse treatment, community service, with electronic monitoring and boot camp used relatively infrequently as a condition of probation.

Data are not available regarding the distribution of probation and parole conditions among white-collar offenders. Even so, given the nature of white-collar offending and the characteristics or white-collar criminals, some conditions would intuitively seem more appropriate for white-collar offenders than other conditions. For instance, because most white-collar offenders do not have substance abuse

FIGURE 5.2. FEDERAL OFFENDERS UNDER COMMUNITY SUPERVISION WITH SPECIAL CONDITIONS, BY TYPE OF SPECIAL CONDITION, 1992–1996.

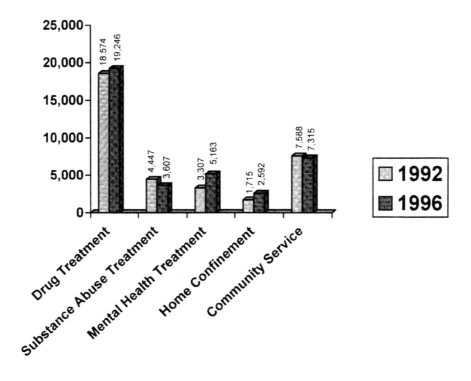

Source: Adapted from *Trends in Community Supervision of Federal Offenders* (1997).

TABLE 5.4
**CONDITIONS OF SENTENCES OF ADULT PROBATIONERS,
BY SEVERITY OF OFFENSE (1995)**

		Severity of Offense	
Condition of Sentence	*Total*	*Felony*	*Misdemeanor*
Any condition	98.6	98.4	98.9
Fees, fines, court costs	84.3	84.2	85.1
Supervision fee	61.0	63.9	59.8
Fines	55.8	47.4	67.9
Court costs	54.5	56.4	54.5
Restitution to victim	30.3	39.7	17.6
Boot camp	0.5	0.8	0.1
Electronic monitoring	2.9	3.2	2.0
House arrest without electronic monitoring	0.8	1.1	0.5
Curfew	0.9	1.6	0
Restriction on movement	4.2	5.3	2.9
Restrictions	21.1	24.0	16.0
No contact with	10.4	11.8	8.2
Driving restrictions	5.3	4.3	5.8
Community service	25.7	27.3	24.0
Substance abuse treatment	38.2	48.1	23.7
Mandatory drug	32.5	43.0	17.1
Remain alcohol/drug free	8.1	10.4	5.2
Substance abuse treatment	41.0	37.5	45.7
Alcohol	29.2	21.3	41.0
Drug	23.0	28.3	14.8
Other treatment	17.9	16.1	20.9
Sex offenders program	2.5	3.9	0.2
Psychiatric/psychological counseling	7.1	8.9	4.7
Other counseling	9.2	4.4	16.4
Employment and training	40.3	45.4	34.4
Employment	34.7	40.9	27.3
Education/training	15.0	15.5	15.1
Other special conditions	16.5	19.0	12.6
Number of probationers	2,558,981	1,470,696	982,536

Source: Bonczar, T. P. (1997).

problems, one would expect few of them to be assigned this condition. Of course, some white-collar offenders will need substance abuse treatment, but most will not. From a restorative justice framework, restitution and community service seem to make sense as well as less punitive sanctions that allow offenders to maintain employment (e.g., house arrest with electronic monitoring).

Community Service and White-Collar Offenders

Community service conditions entail offenders providing some form of service for a particular organization or the community at large. In some cases, the service is provided as a form of restitution with the victim receiving the wages the offender would have received while in other cases the wages are waived for the good of the organization receiving the services. Community service has a number of benefits including the following:

- It is more rehabilitative than jail.
- It is cheap.
- The offender can become a part of the community and make amends.
- It facilitates re-entry into the community for those who were institutionalized.
- The community benefits from the services.
- The offender will learn about different groups (Larsen, 1989; Miller, 1996; Sangree & Becerra, 1999).

Some see community service as too lenient for offenders. Those who perform community service activities, however, note that the loss of time (e.g., away from one's family, social activities, free time, etc.) is especially punitive (Larsen, 1989). In the words of Jerome Miller, codirector of the National Center on Institutions and Alternatives, for white-collar offenders sentenced to community service, "We can make the punishment just as distasteful [as jail]" (Otter, 1985: n.p.). More in line with restorative ideals, one judge applauds community service on the grounds that the condition "is forced responsibility [that] does something for the person doing it, the defendant. . .[and] for the taxpayers" (Levin, 1990: 1C).

Although the condition can be given to any offender, it is especially useful for white-collar offenders. Consider the following examples:

- A computer engineer set up computer training programs for nonprofit agencies in one community (Larsen, 1989).
- Accountants were ordered to dispense free tax advice to community members (O'Donnell, 1992).
- After being convicted of occupational offenses, meat packing business owners were ordered to hire some paroled felons (O'Donnell, 1992).
- A physician was ordered to provide free medical services to indigent clients after defrauding the Medicaid system (Rosoff et al., 1998).
- In July 1989, Oliver North was sentenced to twelve-hundred hours of community service to work with drug plagued youth in an inner- city neighborhood in Washington D.C. When leaving the courthouse, he commented that he looked forward to "enlisting in the war on drugs" (Bennett, 1989: 19).

In line with restorative justice ideals, two principles guide the way community service conditions should be used. First, the victim and the community must be given a voice in determining which services are needed in order to ensure that the service experience is valuable to the community (Bazemore & Pranis, 1997). Second, caution must be taken so that offenders are not placed in a position in which they weaken the protection of the community, or commit future offenses. Basically this means that offenders should not be placed in positions that are related to their offenses—an embezzler should not be given a community service position in which money is handled (Larsen, 1989).

Problems with community service include offenders not showing up and offenders cheating on their hours (Sangree and Becerra, 1999). As far as showing up is concerned, given the hard work ethic of most white-collar offenders, it would seem that "no shows" would be more common among conventional offenders than among white-collar offenders. Cheating on hours, however, is likely equally distributed between both groups of offenders. Many likely recall Leona Helmsley's community service efforts. She was supposed to stuff envelopes for charity, but she got her maid to do it instead. When supervisors learned of her cheating, she was given an extra 150 hours of community service (Casey, 1995). With appropriate supervision, the likelihood of offenders cheating on the hours is minimized. House arrest with electronic monitoring is among the strictest form of supervision available as a condition of probation or parole.

Electronic Monitoring and White-Collar Offenders

House arrest with electronic monitoring has become a popular sanction since its inception in Florida in 1984. Used for all types of nonviolent offenders (conventional and white-collar alike), the sanction entails having offenders wear a bracelet or anklet with a device hooked up to their telephone that alerts officials when the offender is not home when he or she is supposed to be. Many different kinds of monitoring devices exist, but the similarity among the devices is that they allow officials to monitor offenders' whereabouts with a high degree of reliability. The option is used either as a pretrial detention method or as a method to monitor convicted offenders.

One of the issues that comes up when white-collar offenders are sentenced to house arrest with electronic monitoring is that the sanction is seen as too lenient, and not punitive enough, because white-collar offenders are permitted to live in such plush surroundings. Two points counter this criticism. First, if restorative justice ideals are being sought, it is more important to have a sanction that promotes accountability rather than pain, and this is an alternative that affords offenders the ability to maintain their employment, thereby giving them a better opportunity to pay their debt to their victims and to society.

Second, recognizing that public demand plays a role in both retributive and restorative justice ideals, it is important to note that house arrest with electronic monitoring is truly experienced as a type of punishment among offenders. Surveys of 49 electronically monitored offenders by Payne and Gainey (1998) revealed that monitored offenders will experience pains of imprisonment similar to those discussed by Sykes (1958), and they will also experience a separate set of pains that are unique to the monitoring experience (see Table 5.5). Furthermore, these pains might be experienced differently among white-collar offenders. Briefly, the following list highlights the way white-collar offenders would be expected to experience house arrest with electronic monitoring:

- *Deprivation of autonomy* is experienced in that white-collar offenders must give up their freedom and abide by controls and restrictions. Accustomed to being in charge, loss of autonomy may be particularly difficult for white-collar offenders.
- *Deprivation of goods and services* is experienced because white-collar offenders will not be able to have access to the same kinds of goods and services as nonmonitored offenders.
- *Deprivation of liberty* occurs when white-collar offenders lose civil liberties such as the right to vote. This may be particularly difficult for those offenders for whom politics played a central role in their lives.
- *Deprivation of heterosexual relations* occurs among monitored white-collar offenders when the loss of status contributes to intimacy problems between the offender and his or her spouse.
- *Monetary costs* are experienced by all offenders in that they are expected to pay a fee to offset the costs of the program. This may actually be harder for conventional offenders who have less money.
- *Family effects* are experienced by white-collar offenders when the family loses its lifestyle, status, or other material goods as a result of the conviction. In addition, having the offender home all of the time is often a difficult adjustment for family members.
- *Watching others effects* are experienced when offenders have to watch their family members or peers do things that they are unable to do.
- *Bracelet effects* are experienced when the anklet or bracelet feels invasive, as if it is interfering in the individuals' sense of self. This is particularly problematic for female offenders and may pose problems in the workplace for all offenders.

Of course, one would imagine that house arrest would be easier in plush accommodations as opposed to some poverty-stricken apartment. The fact remains that this is a sanction that is punitive and should meet the public's demand for punishment, but at the same time, the offender's ability to stay in the community increases white-collar offenders' ability to pay back their victims. Because different types of offenders may experience this sanction and all of the other sanctions differently, tips are offered in the next section for corrections professionals supervising and treating white-collar offenders.

TABLE 5.5
PAINS OF ELECTRONIC MONITORING AND WHITE-COLLAR OFFENDERS

Pain	What it Means	White-Collar Offender Experience
Deprivation of autonomy	Electronically monitored offenders lose their freedom and have very little control over decisions about movement.	White-collar offenders would be permitted to leave home only for work, medical reasons, probation officer visits, and so on.
Deprivation of goods/services	Electronically monitored offenders are not permitted to do activities outside of the home that others take for granted.	White-collar offenders would lose their social activity and would not be permitted to shop, eat out, or do other things without approval.
Deprivation of liberty	Electronically monitored offenders many of their rights, with some losing their right to vote.	White-collar offenders would experience these same losses.
Deprivation of heterosexual relations	Electronically monitored offenders do not lose their ability to have relations with others, but these relations are certainly influenced by the sanction.	Because of the loss of status experienced by the offender, partners may also lose status, thereby potentially influencing the relationship.
Monetary costs	Electronicall monitored offenders usually have to pay to be on the sanction.	White-collar offenders would experience the same losses as conventional offenders here, though relatively speaking this may be more of a cost for conventional offenders.
Family effects	The family members of electronicall monitored offenders must change their actions when someone in their home is monitored.	The loss of status would be experienced by the entire family, and some may actually lose their home as well as other taken for granted comforts.
Watching other's effects	Electronically monitored offenders see others engaging in activities that they would like to be doing.	White-collar offenders would experience the same losses.
Bracelet effects	Electronically monitored offenders often complain about having to wear the bracelet.	Offenders who are working would find the most discomfort with the bracelet, expecially if it was noticeable.

Source: Adapted from Payne & Gainey (1998).

TIPS FOR SUPERVISING AND TREATING WHITE-COLLAR OFFENDERS

TIP #1—PSYCHOLOGICAL THREATS ARE USEFUL IN GETTING OFFEND-ERS TO ABIDE BY RULES OF PRISON OR CONDITIONS OF PROBATION OR PAROLE. When white-collar offenders are experiencing a punishment, they adjust to the punishment and do not want the punishment to get any worse. Consequently, psychological pressure is an effective strategy to gain compliance among white-collar inmates, probationers, and parolees (Andresky, 1984; Nadler, 1992). For those in minimum security prisons, misbehavior can result in movement to a more restrictive higher security environment full of more dangerous offenders (Pollick, 1998). Said one white-collar offender, "Just the thought of being . . . put in a higher security prison was enough to keep me in line" (Frayler, 2000: 049).

It goes without saying that psychological threats are more effective when offenders are in environments they already see as safe. For white-collar offenders being institutionalized, it is important that classification officials find safe places for the offenders to spend their time (Castlebury, 2001). This is even more important when dealing with high profile white-collar inmates. Mike Countz, director of classification for the Texas Department of Corrections, says, "You focus less on what the big-name inmate might do, and worry more that some misguided no-name inmate will try to grab 15 minutes of fame by making a hit on some high-profile inmate" (Castlebury, 2001: n.p.). Consequently, when placed in a safe environment, white-collar inmates will want to stay there, as opposed to a higher security prison, and many will respond to fear of transfer as a way to gain compliance. Corrections professionals will generally not need to vocalize threats, as they likely already exist in the minds of most white-collar inmates.

TIP #2—DO NOT TAKE FRUSTRATIONS OUT ON WHITE-COLLAR INMATES IN ORDER TO AVOID BECOMING INTIMIDATED BY THEM. Many white-collar offenders tend to be charismatic, smart, and persuasive. Solomon (1998) warned that corrections professionals must not become seduced or intimidated by white-collar personalities. One probation supervisor tells his probation officers the following: "These guys spend more money on shoes than you make in a year. Can you handle that?" (Solomon, 1998: 3). In attempting to avoid intimidation, it is important that corrections officials not overcompensate and treat white-collar offenders more harshly than other offenders. As one warden said, "They come here as punishment, not to be punished" (Jacobs, 1998: A15).

TIP #3–DO NOT ASSUME THAT THEY ARE NOT EXPERIENCING PUNISHMENT. Whether institutionalized or under community supervision, white-collar offenders are being punished, and it is important that correctional professionals recognize that their sanction is experienced as punitive. This is especially important given the misconceptions that members of the public have about federal minimum security prisons, which are seen as too lenient (Sciacca, 1997). Given the label "Club Fed" to describe the supposedly posh environment, five themes about federal minimum security prisons abound in the media:

1. No discipline takes place in these prisons.
2. Individuals do not work when they are incarcerated.
3. Offenders have no remorse for their misdeeds.
4. Sexual immorality is common in these institutions.
5. The lack of security threatens the safety of all of the public (Freeman, 2000:29).

Of course, these themes are inaccurate portrayals of federal institutions. Here are two quotes from the print media that tacitly illustrate these inaccurate themes:

1. "The rich and powerful . . . are sifted out from the riffraff and accorded their own form of punishment" (Bart, 1983: 22).
2. "The deluxe lock-up is reached along a winding road lined with shady oaks draped in Spanish moss and magnolia trees surrounded by planters with purple, pink, and white periwinkles. The hedges are neatly clipped and freshly mown lawns surround tennis courts, softball diamonds, and a soccer field" (Balfour, 2000: n.p.).

Corrections professionals must keep in mind that white-collar offenders feel the pains of confinement, even in minimum security institutions where they still lack privacy, autonomy, freedom, and so on (Andresky, 1984; Nadler, 1992).

It is not surprising that minimum security prison authorities and inmates scoff at references suggesting that some institutions are worthy of the club fed label (Kaczor, 1999). Here's a sampling of their responses to suggestions that minimum security institutions are too lenient:

- "People have the totally wrong idea if they think all they'll have to do at Danbury is play tennis and work on their tans" (Andresky, 1984: 114).
- "There is no club fed about it. [This] is the ultimate loss of privacy" (Council, 1997: 1).
- "Everybody thinks it's club fed, that it's a country club. But it can't be pleasant, because the loss of one's freedom is so horrible you can't imagine it unless it happens to you (Lore, 1992: 1F).
- "They complain that we have everything. If they want to trade places with me, I'll trade places" (Ayed, 2001: n.p.).
- "Sure, we've got one tennis court—for 632 inmates" (Bacon, 1988: n.p.).
- "Inmates are not coddled. You can't leave at night. You can't see your wife and kids when you'd like. To me, that's not a country club (Bacon, 1988: n.p.).
- "If this is club fed, we don't find too many people waiting in line to get in" (*Washington Post*, 1989: 03).

Prison expert Hans Toch is particularly offended by the club fed stereotype and notes, "This country-club reputation is a silly myth" (Wilkie, 1990: A1). The problem with the country club image is that the general deterrent potential of these sanctions is minimized. Why would white-collar offenders fear incarceration in a country club? Some convicted white-collar offenders have actually thought that they could bring golf clubs and cell phones with them to prison (Cutter, 2001). It is incumbent on corrections professionals to remember that white-collar offenders are experiencing punishment, whether it is in a minimum security prison, on house arrest, or by fulfilling community service requirements. This relates to a fourth tip.

TIP #4—IN ORDER TO GENERATE MORE UNDERSTANDING ABOUT THE WAY WHITE-COLLAR OFFENDERS EXPERIENCE PUNISHMENT, COR-

RECTIONS OFFICIALS SHOULD TAKE MEASURES TO EDUCATE THE PUB-
LIC ABOUT THEIR MISCONCEPTIONS. Involving correctional professionals in educating the public has been seen as a viable strategy by
a number of experts (Andring 1993; Gondles 1998; Hawk 1994). In
terms of the punishment experiences of white-collar offenders,
members of the public should be informed about five concerns.
First, corrections professionals should share the way that incarceration truly punishes white-collar offenders, regardless of where the
incarceration occurs. Second, corrections professionals should educate the public about the punitive and rehabilitative appeal of various community-based sanctions for white-collar offenders. Third,
from a restorative justice perspective, corrections professionals
should educate the public about their possible involvement in the
response to white-collar misconduct. Fourth, and also in line with
restorative justice ideals, corrections professionals should educate
the public to confront myths individuals have about hiring former
offenders (these myths are discussed later). Former offenders with
jobs are in a better position to make amends with victims. Finally, in
order to strengthen the deterrent value of punishments given to
white-collar offenders, corrections professionals should educate the
public about the losses experienced by white-collar offenders. Strategies
to educate include educational campaigns, press releases, prison
tours, and speaking engagements.

TIP #5–CORRECTIONS PROFESSIONALS SHOULD MAKE EFFORTS TO
OVERCOME WHITE-COLLAR OFFENDERS' DENIAL WHEN APPROPRIATE.
It has been established that white-collar offenders are notorious for
offering various denials or excuses for their misconduct. Not all
counselors and psychologists agree that individuals must overcome
their denial in order to recover fully. However, in terms of restorative justice, it would be important to make efforts to get offenders to
accept responsibility. According to a supervisor of white-collar
offenders in a Baltimore halfway house, white-collar offenders "need
to recognize they've done something wrong and resolve not to do it
again" (*Baltimore Sun*, 1999: 1A). Another director of a counseling
program in a federal program seems to agree as she stated, "they
must come to terms with their pasts and place blame squarely where
it belongs–on themselves" (*WVSOM Magazine*, 2001: n.p.).

The problem is that it is not easy to get white-collar offenders, who
have worn their cloak of denial throughout their offenses, to admit

they did anything wrong. Corrections consultant Anne Seymour (1998: 358) wrote, "For some offenders, accountability is much more difficult than retributive punishment. Taking responsibility for wrongdoing and making amends for harm caused can make incarceration or detention seem like the easier alternative." Denial can be overcome. One author cites five steps to overcome denial: (1) assess the client, (2) deal with the involuntary nature of the client, (3) challenge false beliefs, (4) find a problem clients will work on, and (5) develop a treatment plan (Harris, 1995: 47).

A range of treatment plans are available to assist in overcoming denial. Some say it is easier for offenders to overcome denial in group treatment settings where the group leader can use "repetition, control, and peer pressure to get offenders to drop their excuses" (Czunder & Mueller, 1987: 74). Strategies to be used in the group setting include the following:

- Making an emotional appeal on the behalf of victims.
- Creating an atmosphere of fairness.
- Involving family members of offenders in groups.
- Exchanging films or news articles of traumatic events.
- Encouraging members of the group to share their observations of the pain they caused others. (Czunder & Mueller, 1987: 74).

Denial can be overcome, but it may take time and resolve on the part of the corrections official treating the offender.

TIP #6–ESTABLISH A PURPOSE FOR WHITE-COLLAR OFFENDERS, ESPECIALLY THOSE WHO ARE INCARCERATED. For white-collar offenders, especially those who are incarcerated, one of the most difficult adjustments they have to make is getting used to the loss of status in an environment that is so downright boring to them. In order to help them cope with their status loss and environment, it is recommended that efforts are made to help them find a purpose or meaning for their lives. Current and former white-collar inmates are quick to cite the importance of developing a sense of purpose. Former Louisiana Insurance Commission Sherman Bernard, who spent time in a federal prison in Alabama, said that on his first night in prison he "started crying, I mean really crying" (Roig-Franzia, 2000: n.p.). When he found a sense of purpose in sweeping the floors and changing light bulbs, he was better able to cope. Another white-collar offender advised fellow inmates to do something with their time saying, "It means something. At least when you get home you can say, 'Hey, I didn't waste my time'" (Crable, 1995: 15).

Prison officials also recognize why it is important to give purpose to white-collar offender's daily routines. Said one prison official about white-collar offenders, "We want to keep them busy all the time to release all the stress they have" (Foy, 1995: n.p.). In a similar way, describing this need for a sense of purpose, Warden Burl Cain (1998: 2-39) wrote:

> Human garbage is created when inmates are not provided with opportunities to express their creativity and feel that they are contributing to something worthwhile. However, unlike garbage, you cannot throw human beings away. You will need to be creative and recycle.

White-collar inmates have been used in creative ways to instill this sense of purpose. In one federal prison camp, a former stock market employee taught a class on investing to inmates. They each got $10,000 fictitious dollars to invest (Wilkie, 1990). In another prison, an investor taught an economics course to inmates (Andresky, 1984). Certainly undereducated inmates will, at least in principle, benefit from having educated offenders around them (Douthat, 1989).

A problem that arises is that it is not always easy to find ways for white-collar inmates to use their skills in ways that would not be disruptive to prison routine. A former judge wanted a job in the law library, but he was advised "that his presence in the law library would create too much of an attraction and would disrupt prison routine" (Call, 2001: 491). There are other ways, however, to establish a sense of purpose in white-collar inmates. For example, a former inmate advises that white-collar inmates: (1) establish goals for themselves in prison (2) keep a journal of their thoughts and experiences, (3) practice clean hygiene, and (4) involve themselves in any available education and recreation programs (Tayoun, 2000). Another white-collar inmate found his sense of purpose by sharing his passion of reading with other inmates. He said,

> For me, reading is not escaping from reality, but choosing an enhanced reality in which to live. One of the most precious gifts I can give to fellow prisoners is my passion for books. A great satisfaction during my incar-

> ceration has been awakening some of the African American prisoners to
> their own literacy heritage through earlier black writers like Richard
> Wright and James Baldwin. Sharing some of the moments connected with
> books can make life more tolerable in some pretty intolerable conditions,
> (Gillies, 2000: 79)

Tolerable living for inmates translates to easier supervision for corrections professionals.

TIP #7–USE WHITE-COLLAR OFFENDERS TO TEACH OTHERS ABOUT THE RISK OF WHITE-COLLAR OFFENDING. This tip relates directly to the previous point but is broader in that it suggests that white-collar inmates' skills can be used for the good of individuals inside, and outside the institution. White-collar inmates can be used to educate the public through prison tours or guest speaking assignments.

Tours are becoming increasingly common as a way to educate individuals about the risks of white-collar misconduct. University of Maryland Accounting Professor Stephen Loeb has his Masters of Business Administration (MBA) students visit the Federal Correctional Institution in Cumberland, Maryland. Referred to as a "Scared Straight Program for Yuppies," on a recent visit, a former assistant district attorney serving five years for occupational misdeeds told the group, "The pain, the sorrow, the fracturing of human spirit, it's all here." (*People Weekly*, 2000: 95). Dr. Blain McCormick, a professor at Baylor University, also has students in his Strategic Management and Business Policy class visit a prison to talk to inmates about white-collar crime. The professor commented specifically on the way students see firsthand the consequences of unethical behavior. He said,

> Just . . . entering the prison opened students' eyes to some harsh realities.
> No wallets, purses, or keys were allowed inside the unit, and we had to
> turn over our driver's licenses as we entered–which gives you an uneasy
> feeling that you are now somehow vulnerable, (Corwin & McCormick,
> 1999: 11)

In a more structured program, halfheartedly referred to as "Scared Straight: The Club Fed Edition" (see Bravin, 2000), a program developed by James T. Martinoff involved MBA students from Pepperdine University visiting Nellis Federal Prison Camp near Las Vegas. During one prison tour at Nellis, two MBA students immediately called their businesses to tell them to change the way things were being done. Reportedly, it is not uncommon to have students leave their jobs for more ethical jobs after going on the tour (Kisken, 1999). Professor Martinoff suggests that his program provides "an ethical anchor for making future business decisions" (Bravin, 2001: n.p.).

Related to Professor Martinoff's tours, the Ethical Management Consultant's Group was created to help get the message to organizations whose employees would otherwise not receive information about the risks of white-collar crime. Members of the consultants group, some of whom are former white-collar inmates, provide workshops and lectures about ethical conduct to organizations. The former offenders are given a small monthly salary, much of which is used to pay restitution for their prior offenses (Ettore, 1994).

In other places, white-collar inmates are permitted to leave their institutions in order to serve as guest speakers in college classrooms. Susquehanna University Accounting Professor Richard Davis has recruited white-collar inmates to speak to his business law class for several recent years. The inmates enjoy the opportunity to do something different and realize that they may actually help to keep students from "stepping out of line" (Brown, 1998). According to Professor Davis, "what really grabs [the students] is that these guys had everything the students dreamed of obtaining. Now they have nothing" (Brown, 1998: 8).

Colleges and universities across the United States are increasingly using incarcerated offenders as business ethics lecturers. Given that these offenses are seen as rational offenses planned out in advance, the assumption underlying the lectures is that students will think twice about engaging in occupational misconduct. In full, there are four benefits, each relating to restorative justice ideals, of using inmates to educate the public: (1) crime is possibly deterred, (2) relations are improved between the offender and the community, (3) myths about the punishment of white-collar offenders are dispelled, and (4) inmates feel a sense of purpose.

TIP #8–TRADITIONAL PROGRAMS CAN BE USED IN SOME CASES, BUT NEWER PROGRAMS MAY ALSO BE NEEDED TO ACHIEVE RESTORATIVE JUSTICE IDEALS. Many of the programs used for conventional offenders can be used to treat white-collar offenders. These programs may not always work for white-collar offenders for at least three reasons.

First, the typical white-collar offender tends to be older than conventional offenders, and conventional programs are generally not designed for older offenders (Gallagher, 1990; Weisburd & Waring, 2001; Wheeler et al., 1988). Second, many variations of drug programs are available for conventional offenders, but the vast majority of white-collar offenders do not have substance abuse problems. Third, their level of education makes many of the conventional education programs useless for white-collar inmates (Knapp, 1996).

Despite the fact that conventional programs are not always useful for white-collar offenders, newer programs related to restorative justice ideals would seem to be particularly applicable for dealing with white-collar offenders. Three in particular include peer tutoring programs, victim-impact classes, and victim-offender mediation programs.

Regarding peer tutoring programs, to deal with the high number of illiterate and learning disabled offenders, in the early 1980s, the Maryland State Department of Education developed a peer tutoring program in which trained inmates would help other inmates learn to read. The idea of a peer tutoring program originated in a Right to Read grant given to the Johns Hopkins Reading Center in 1980. Steurer (1998: 104) pointed out that the grant originally entailed offering tutoring at adult education sites throughout the state, but "correctional institutions were added as an afterthought." Volunteers were trained how to teach, offer one-on-one tutoring, and use positive motivation techniques. Though not designed for white-collar offenders, the fact that many of them already have a respectable educational background, combined with their need to find a purpose, would make programs such as this one useful in helping them to give back to the community.

Victim-impact classes are strategies that allow victims to teach offenders about the consequences of victimization. These classes also encourage offenders to accept responsibility and are seen as useful because they create a link between justice agencies and victim service agencies (Burnley et al., 1998). Burnley et al. (1998) cited research suggesting that those who take victim-impact classes are more likely to pay their restitution in full than other offenders are. Because white-collar offenders often justify their actions on the grounds that no one was hurt, these classes would certainly open their eyes to the consequences of their misdeeds.

Victim mediation programs are programs in which victims are given the opportunity to meet with offenders in order to tell them the kinds of losses they experienced. The goal of these programs is not settlement, but a signed restitution agreement often results from the mediation (Burnley et al., 1998). These programs, as well as the victim-impact classes, are most useful in white-collar crime cases when the victim is an individual rather than a business. Moreover, giving the victim a role in the justice process helps to meet restorative ideals.

TIP #9–DO NOT ASSUME THAT THEY CANNOT BE REHABILITATED OR THAT THEY ARE NOT IN NEED OF TREATMENT. Because white-collar offenders are different from conventional offenders, many assume that they are not in need of treatment. Interviews with 51 federal judges who tried a significant number of cases "revealed virtually no concern with individual rehabilitation of the offender" (Wheeler et al., 1988: 132). Asked about the purposes for imprisoning white-collar offenders, one judge was quoted saying, "Prisons are simply not going to rehabilitate white-collar offenders . . . so I'm not concerned about rehabilitation" (Mann et al., 1980: 482). Furthermore, when they are sanctioned in the community, white-collar offenders "are already at the point which the agency hopes to bring its average clients" (Benson, 1982: 54).

Taken together, four perceptions limit the ability of sanctions to help white-collar offenders:

1. It is believed that they will not need different kinds of responses than other offenders.
2. It is believed that they are not in need of aftercare or halfway houses after incarceration.
3. It is believed that they do not need treatment programs.
4. It is believed that they are not in need of services or counseling (Andresky, 1984).

Not only are they in need of aftercare, counseling, or treatment programs, they can actually benefit from services offered in the community or in the institution where they are incarcerated. Indeed, even incarceration can serve as a positive experience in white-collar offenders' lives. Describing his meeting with a white-collar inmate, attorney Allen Ellis told the *Corporate Crime Reporter* (2000: n.p.) the following:

> There he was, dressed in Khakis. He looked fantastic. He must have lost twenty pounds. He had a flat stomach. I said, "Dave, you look terrific." And he looked at me and said, "Allen, you look like hell." He said, "I don't drink. I cut down on smoking. I exercise everyday. It is like rehab. I'm reading the great book that I never had the time to read. The government has taken away sixteen months of my life. I'm going to add three years back on the back end through healthy living."

Other testimonials of the ability of prison or jail experiences to change white-collar offenders should help to establish that incarceration can serve as a positive experience for some offenders:

> In prison, you have a lot of time to think about what is really important. And, I can tell you it's not the clothes, cars, and trips that I convinced myself I needed. It's family—and having a sense of purpose. . . . As strange as it may seem . . . I'm more proud of myself now than I've been in years [white-collar offender halfway through a ten year sentence], (Hansen, 2000: n.p.).

> It was probably one of the best experiences for me, because I'd lost all of my money and my life had fallen apart. It was time to reassess my life. Don't get me wrong—I hated it, I hated it, I hated it. But I tried to do what I needed to do, to get my life back together [white-collar inmate reflecting back on his prison sentence]. (Flannery, 1998: A7)

Certainly, many white-collar offenders will need some sort of treatment in addition to their sentence. Some will need to learn discipline, self-respect, and what it means to be responsible (Jacobs, 1998), whereas others will need help coping with the enormous amount of shame and embarrassment they caused themselves and their families.

TIP #10–ASSISTANCE MAY BE NEEDED GETTING A DIFFERENT JOB. Because most convicted white-collar offenders will lose their jobs, assistance may be needed finding employment. White-collar offenders' employment strengths include the fact that they have strong work habits, with many being workaholics (Andresky, 1984). Their weakness lies in the fact that they have been convicted of an offense, and employers do not always have favorable attitudes towards former offenders. Henry and Odiorme (1989) cited specific myths that employers have about offenders:

- All convicts are alike.
- Ex-prisoners have no useful job skills.
- Educated people never go to prison.
- Only convicted criminals are offenders.
- Ex-convicts cannot hold a job.
- Laws generally prohibit hiring former offenders.
- Once employed, exoffenders need special monitoring.

Correctional professionals should help white-collar inmates seeking employment to understand that these are the myths they will have to overcome in their job search.

It is not surprising that research shows that employers are most willing to hire offenders whose crime was unrelated to their job (Albright & Deng, 1996). Individuals convicted of bank embezzlement will never work in a bank again. Still, in some states, businesses can earn up to $2,400 dollars a year in tax credits for each convicted felon employed by the business. The Worker's Opportunity Tax Credit varies according to the number of hours employed by the exfelon and his or her salary. To protect against white-collar offenses committed by the exfelon, employers can buy a bond from the federal government stipulating that the government will pay between $5,000 and $10,000 if the individual steals from the company. Those helping former inmates to find employment will want to make sure that businesses are aware of these options (*Omaha World Herald*, 1999).

The importance of employment cannot be understated for white-collar offenders. Employed offenders will be less likely to recidivate, and they are in a position to pay back their victims. Community protection and restitution are central to restorative justice ideals.

TIP #11—DO NOT ASSUME THAT BECAUSE THEY ARE DIFFERENT FROM CONVENTIONAL CRIMINALS THAT THEY WILL BE MORE HONEST THAN OTHER OFFENDERS. Study after study shows that criminal justice officials have "great personal sympathy" toward white-collar offenders because they can relate to the offender in terms of their status and career aspirations (Rackmill, 1992). Said one judge, "I guess it is true that I can probably better understand the white-collar defendant. He is more like me. . . . I guess I do believe that white-collar defendants are more sensitive to and more affected by a prison experience" (Wheeler et al., 1988: 68). Recall from Chapter 4, however, that some white-collar inmates may continue to use the trust they are afforded to commit various rule infractions while incarcerated.

From interviews with probation officers, Benson (1982: 52) concluded that "an affinity exists between the life styles of officers and [white-collar] offenders." Benson further noted that white-collar probationers are less likely to create problems for probation officers than other conventional probationers. He wrote:

> The potential areas of misunderstanding that arise between probation officers and ordinary offenders do not develop with white-collar offenders. They are not likely to associate with persons engaging in criminal activity. They are likely to be employed, to support their dependants, and to maintain reasonable lives. (Benson, 1982: 52)

One might say that white-collar probationers are easier to supervise than conventional probationers are. Probation officers must keep in mind, however, that the offenders were convicted of an offense, and they must adhere to any restrictions that were part of the sentence. Placing too much trust in offenders because they are easier to supervise could backfire.

TIP #12–SOME WHITE-COLLAR OFFENDERS WILL BE HIGH PUBLICITY INMATES SO CORRECTIONS PROFESSIONALS SHOULD BE PREPARED TO DEAL WITH THE MEDIA. The very nature of the news business is that what is reported is the exception to the norm. White-collar offenders in prison or jail are certainly the exception, and because many of these offenders, or at least their cases, are known to the public, corrections professionals should expect a certain amount of media attention when white-collar offenders are under correctional supervision. It is important that corrections departments have written policies for dealing with the press in these cases. In Texas, for instance, wardens do not allow the press to conduct interviews with inmates until it has been determined that the offender has adjusted to the incarceration experience (Castlebury, 2001). Because most white-collar offenders will eventually adjust to the prison experience, it is recommended that the press not be granted interviews in the early stages of the white-collar inmate's incarceration. To allow the press access to inmates in the early stages of the incarceration (when inmates are in shock or depressed) could lead to much unneeded negative attention in the media.

TIP #13–DON'T FORGET ABOUT THE FAMILIES OF CONVICTED WHITE-COLLAR INMATES. As with the other tips, this tip is not meant to suggest that the punishment experience is worse for white-collar offenders and their families than it is for other offenders and their families; instead, it is to suggest that the punishment experience is different. Certainly, a number of programs exist to help inmates' families cope with their family members' incarceration. Most of these programs, however, are directed toward the family members of conventional criminals. Consequently, family members of white-collar inmates may find that these programs are not useful in helping to adjust to the different kinds of losses and emotions they experience.

For example, according to Breed (1979), many conventional criminals live in low-cost rentals that are often subsidized by governmental welfare. When sent to prison, their families do not generally lose their homes. He further stated:

> A white-collar man has much to lose, both in financial terms and status. His life is shattered by the offense and subsequent prison sentence. There is little chance of his returning either to the previous occupation that gave him that status or to his previous standard of living. . . . For the white-collar offender the change is considerable, and he is very fortunate indeed if anything of his former life-style remains when he leaves prison. It seems obvious that he must need . . . help to remake his life. . . . Yet the myth remains that he needs very little. (p. 111)

Breed further notes that families of white-collar inmates will often distance themselves from friends and relatives due to the shame and humiliation stemming of the conviction.

Communication between the offender and the family is key. After all, in many situations, the "unshareable financial problem" is seen as a contributing factor to the offense. This means that white-collar offenders were not able to communicate with their families about their financial plight. One prison chaplain recommends that inmates write their family members letters of apology to let the family members know how sorry they really are (Castillo, 1996). In addition, younger family members will have to be told why they have lost their parent, their home, and their lifestyle. One white-collar inmate did this by telling her grandson, "Grandma is on a giant time out"

(Keller, 2000: 311).

TIP #14–RESTORATIVE JUSTICE IDEALS ARE PARTICULARLY USEFUL IN DEALING WITH WHITE-COLLAR OFFENDERS. Punishment alone does virtually no good in terms of a response to white-collar crime. Victims are not satisfied, and the public good is not restored. What needs to happen is offenders need to be made accountable for their offenses, victims need to have a say in recovering from the harm, and strategies need to be taken to protect the community from future offenses. Like other offenders, white-collar offenders should not become hardened by their criminal justice experience; rather, they should be held accountable in a way that satisfies victims and the community at the same time limiting the possibility that the offender will engage in future misconduct. By holding offenders accountable through practices such as restitution, community service, and victim-offender mediation, a more pragmatic response to crime results for victims and the community (Bazemore & Schiff, 2001).

APPLIED CRITICAL THINKING QUESTIONS

1. Why do we punish white-collar offenders?
2. Compare and contrast retributive justice and restorative justice.
3. Which community based sanctions would be most useful for white-collar offenders?
4. How would white-collar offenders experience house arrest, as compared to conventional offenders?
5. How can denial be overcome?
6. Why is it important to establish a sense of purpose in white-collar inmates?
7. What are some myths about hiring former offenders?
8. How can restorative justice ideals be met in punishing white-collar offenders?

Chapter 6

WHITE-COLLAR CRIME AND WHITE-COLLAR TIME: CONCLUDING REMARKS

There is a crime problem in the United States. Most often when individuals think of this problem, they envision the offenses of rape, assault, motor vehicle theft, and other conventional offenses. Less often envisioned as part of this crime problem are white-collar offenses. But, these offenses occur, and the justice system spends a great deal of time prosecuting and convicting white-collar offenders. Convicted white-collar offenders, however, are often seen as if they are in need of the same kinds of supervision and treatment responses as conventional criminals when they are not. Once again, the intent of this book is not to suggest that white-collar offenders should be treated more leniently. Rather, it is to suggest that in some cases, they should be handled differently. Based on the literature on the punishment of white-collar offenders, a number of recommendations for policy and future research can be made.

First, research shows that white-collar offenders will adjust to their incarceration experience (Benson & Cullen, 1988). Consequently, judges who avoid incarcerating white-collar offenders because they believe the adjustment is too difficult are basing their sentencing decisions on false assumptions. However, research also shows that long sentences are not needed for many white-collar offenders. What is best, it is suggested, are split sentences in which offenders receive a short stint of incarceration to meet general deterrence ideals, followed by community-based supervision to help offenders adjust to the loss of their status (Benson, 1985b). This practice has proven to be a success in some states. In New Jersey, for example, some white-collar inmates are placed in the state's Intensive Supervision Parole Program after they have spent some time incarcerated. As part of their release, offenders are expected to maintain employment, keep diaries, perform community service, and pay restitution to victims, each of which are in line with restorative justice ideals,

Second, training received by corrections officials is usually directed toward what is needed to supervise and treat conventional offenders. Not being prepared to supervise and treat white-collar offenders, although they represent a small proportion of the offenders supervised and treated by most corrections professionals, could actually result in these "different" offenders taking up a substantial proportion of the professionals' time. It is important that corrections professionals are prepared to deal with all kinds of offenders.

Third, white-collar offenders need to be given the opportunity to rebuild their lives. A conviction should not be a death sentence for these offenders. At the same time, offenders must be given guidance from corrections professionals to adjust to their loss of status, as well as adjusting to the fact that they will have to regain the trust of their family and the community.

Fourth, restitution is a "key component of restorative justice" (Burnley et al., 1998: n.p.). It seems obvious that, where feasible, victims must be paid back for their losses. Unfortunately, "victims left broke usually take a back seat to those left bleeding" (Roberts, 2000: A1). Certainly restitution cannot be made in all cases, and victims should have a role in deciding whether they want restitution (Burnley et al., 1998).

Fifth, all policy makers must recognize that white-collar crime is quickly becoming an international offense (Pontell & Frid, 2000; Van Alphen, 2001). This internationalization of the problem will be sure to present difficulties in terms of the justice system's response to the offenses. Who has jurisdiction over an offense where the victim resides in the United States, but the offender resides in another country? Where should this offender be punished? What do corrections professionals need to know to respond to these international offenses? These and other questions will need to be answered in the future.

Research still needs to be conducted in a number of areas so that an even better understanding about the way punishment is experienced by white-collar offenders is forthcoming. Most often, research on the punishment of white-collar offenders has focused on whether they recidivate or not. This past research is important, but the actual process of punishment has been virtually ignored. White-collar offenders who are incarcerated should be interviewed at various stages of their incarceration experience to see how the process of incarceration is experienced.

In addition, those who have completed prison or jail sentences should be interviewed to see how they have adapted to the loss of status. One note of caution—it is natural for white-collar offenders to avoid discussing their pasts. One journalist who was working on a story about white-collar inmates contacted 30 former white-collar felons for her story noted: "Understandably, most them told me to get lost. They had done their time and that part of their life was a closed chapter. They had made new lives and did not want to remind anyone of their past" (Loane, 2000: n.p.).

Research should also focus on the experiences of corrections professionals who supervise and treat white-collar offenders. Such research could determine the most effective strategies as well as the strategies that simply do not work. Among other professionals, the input of wardens, classification specialists, counselors, psychologists, correctional officers, probation and parole officers, restitution officers, community service supervisors, and any other professionals who work with convicted white-collar inmates should be sought. The best way to understand how white-collar offenders experience the application of justice is to ask either the offenders themselves or those who are actually meting out justice. Such research would be difficult, time consuming, worthy of a thesis or dissertation, and it would also be rewarding. Perhaps readers thinking about graduate school would want to consider such a study.

REFERENCES

Abelson, N. and J. Balco. 1992. "Keeping the CEO out of Jail." *Risk Management.* 19: 14-17.

Agnew, R. 1985. "A Revised Strain Theory of Delinquency." *Social Forces* 64:151-167.

Agnew, R. 1992. "Foundation for a General Strain Theory of Crime and Delinquency." *Criminology* 30:47–88.

Agnew, R. and A. Peters. 1986. "The Techniques of Neutralization: An Analysis of Predispositional and Situational Factors." *Criminal Justice and Behavior.* 13:81–97.

Akers, R. L. 1991. "Self–Control as a General Theory of Crime." *Journal of Quantitative Criminology.* 7(2):201–211.

Albanese, J. 1999. *Casino Gambling and White-Collar Crime.* American Gaming Association: Washington D.C.

Albrecht, W. S., Howe, K.R., and M.B. Romney. 1984. *Deterring Fraud.* Altamonte Springs, FL: The Institute of Internal Auditors.

Albrecht, W. S. and D.J. Searcy. 2001. "Top 10 Reasons Why Fraud is Increasing in the U.S." *Strategic Finance* 82:58.

Albright, S. and F. Deng. 1996. "Employer Attitudes Towards Hiring Ex-Offenders." *Prison Journal.* 76:118–132.

Allen, P. 1989. "The Verdict's In: Crooks Are Out." *Savings and Community Banker.* 110: 36–43.

Andresky, J. 1984. "Soft Prisons? There's No Such Thing." Forbes. 133: 114–117.

Andring, R. 1993. "A Plan for All Seasons." *Corrections Today.* 55: 26–28.

Apgar, E. 1999. "New Jersey Lags in Incarcerating White-Collar Miscreants." *New Jersey Lawyer.* November 22: 3–5.

Arena, K. 2001. "FBI Arrests Eight in Fraud Scheme." Available online at www.cnn.com. Accessed August 21, 2001.

Arndorfer, J. B. 1995. "Credit Union Scam Artist Draws Record Sentence Massachusetts." *American Banker.* 160(178):2.

Arneklev. B., Cochran, J., & R. Gainey. 1998. "Testing Gottfredson and Hirschi's Low Self-Control Stability Hypothesis: An Exploratory Study." *American Journal of Criminal Justice* 23:107–127.

Associated Press. 2001a. "San Antonio Entrepreneur Facing Investigation." February 22.

Associated Press. 2001b. "Former Operator of Defunct Chain of Private Business Schools Released from Prison." October 11.

Aware Foundation. 2000. "Depression Warning Signs." Available online at www.awarefoundation.org. Accessed October 20, 2001.

Axelrod, D. & C. Kuca. 1998. "White-collar Offenders Most Frequently Asked Questions." *Grid and Bear It.* Available online at www.nacdl.org. Accessed July 28, 2001.

Ayed, N. 2001. "New Institutions May Be Nice, But They're Still in Prison." *The Canadian Press: n.*p.

Bacon, J. 1988. "Federal Prison Camp." Gannett News Service: n.p.

Balfour, M. 2000. "Tax-Fraud May Do Time." *Daily-Dispatch*: n.p.

Ball, A. 2001. "Stearns Gets 30 Years for Scams." *Austin American Statesman.* July 13, B1.

Balsmeier, P. & J. Kelly. 1996. "The Ethics of Sentencing White-Collar Criminals." *Journal of Business Ethics.* 15:143–152.

Baltimore Sun. 1999. "Slightly Chastened, Back at Work." February 16:1A.

Barrett, D. 2001. "Courts Leave White-Collar Cons Addicted to Lying." *New York Post.* February 11:24.

Bart, P. 1983. "Country Club Prisons." *Rolling Stone.* January 22:22–26.

Bayse, D. J. 1995. *Working in Jails and Prisons: Becoming a Part of the Team.* Lanham, MD: American Correctional Association.

Bazemore, G. & K. Pranis. 1997. "Hazards Along the Way." *Corrections Today* 59:84–88.

Bazemore, G. & M. Schiff. (Eds.) 2001. *Restorative Community Justice: Repairing Harm and Transforming Communities.* Cincinnati, OH: Anderson.

Bazemore, G. & M. Umbriet. 1994. *Balanced and Restorative Justice Program Summary.* Office of Juvenile Justice, Delinquency, and Prevention. Washington D.C.: USGPO.

Bazemore, G. & M. Umbriet. 2001. *A Comparison of Four Restorative Conferencing Models.* Washington D.C.: USGPO, Office of Juvenile Justice, Delinquency, and Prevention.

Beccaria, C. 1764. *On Crimes and Punishments.* Philadelphia: Phillip H. Nicklin.

Behar, R. 1998. "Wall Street's Most Ruthless Financial Cannibal." *Fortune.* 137(11): 212–222.

Bennett, J. 1989. "Community Service: A Popular Alternative." *Houston Chronicle.* July 9:19.

Bennetto, J. 1998. "White-Collar Crime Not Seen As Wrong." *The Independent.* September 11:9.

Benson, M. 1982. *Collateral Consequences of Conviction for a White-Collar Crime.* A dissertation completed at University of Illinois at Urbana-Champaign.

Benson, M. 1985a. "Denying the Guilty Mind." *Criminology* 23:589–599.

Benson, M. 1985b. "White-Collar Offenders Under Community Supervision." *Justice Quarterly* 2:429–438.

Benson, M. & F. Cullen. 1988. "The Special Sensitivity of White-collar Offenders to Prison." *Journal of Criminal Justice* 16:207–215.

Benson, M. & E. Moore. 1992. "Are White-collar Offenders and Common Offenders the Same?" *Journal of Research in Crime and Delinquency* 29: 251–272.

Bonczar, T. P. 1997. *Characteristics of Adults on Probation, 1995.* Washington, DC: USGPO, Bureau of Justice Statistics, U.S. Dept. of Justice.

Bonnvissuto, K. 2001. "Net Latest Snare for Senior Scams." *Crain's Cleveland Business.* July 30:17.

Boothby, J. & T. Durham. 1999. "Screening for Depression in Prisoners Using the Beck Depression Inventory." *Criminal Justice and Behavior.* 26:107–114.

Boss, M. S. & B. George. 1992. "Challening Conventional Views of White-Collar Crime." *Criminal Law Bulletin* 24:32–58.

Braithwaite, J. 1992. "Poverty, Power, and White-Collar Crime." In *White-Collar Crime Reconsidered*, edited by K. Schlegel and D. Weisburd. Boston, MA: Northeastern University Press.

Bravin, J. 2000. "Class Learns Ethics With Conviction." *Wall Street Journal Europe.* October 11:23.

Bravin, J. 2001. "Jailed Executives Teach Ethics to MBA Students." *Wall Street Journal.* Accessed September 20, 2001.

Breed, B. 1979. *White-Collar Bird.* London: John Clare Books.

Brewer, S. 1999. "Alzheimer's Victim Robbed of Life Savings." *Houston Chronicle.* November 5:37.

Brostoff, S. 1994. "Crime Bill Cracks Down on Insurance Fraud." *National Underwriter* 36(3):1.

Brown, J. 1998. "The Wrong Kind of Pinstripes." *Business Week.* November 2:8.

Bureau of Prisons. 2002. *BOP Homepage.* Available online at www.bop.gov. Accessed March 2, 2002.

Burnley, J. N., Edmunds, C., Gaboury, M., & A. Seymour. 1998. *1998 National Victim Assistance Academy* Washington DC: USGPO, Office for Victims of Crime. U.S. Department of Justice.

Cain, B. 1998. "Basic Prison 101 for Wardens." In *A View from the Trenches*, edited by E. Rhine. Lanham, MD: American Correctional Association.

Calavita, K., Pontell, H. N., & R. Tillman. 1997. *Big Money Crime: Fraud and Politics in the Savings and Loan Crisis.* Berkeley, CA: University of California Press.

Call, J. E. 2001. "A Prominent Judge Goes to Prison." *Legal Studies Forum.* 25:489–506.

Casey, C. 1995. "Notorious Success–Community Service Celebrities." *Star Tribune Newspaper.* November 11:3F.

Castillo, G. 1996. *My Life Between the Cross and Bars.* Shalimar, FL: G & M Publications.

Castlebury, G. 2001. "A Security Concern for Texas Prisons." *Corrections Today.* Available online at www.corrections.com/aca. Accessed October 21, 2001.

Cauther, J. 2001. "Internet Fraud." *FBI Law Enforcement Bulletin* 70(5):13.

Chaudron. D. 1994. "Mood Disorders." *HR Focus* 71(10):9–10.

Claybrook, J. 1986. "White–Collar Crime–Corporate Misconduct is More Abuse than Street Crime." *Trial* April:35–36.

Clinard, M. 1983. *Corporate Ethics and Crime: The Role of Middle Management.* Beverly Hills, CA: Sage.

Cohen, A. 1955. *Delinquent Boys: The Culture of the Gang.* New York: Free Press.

Cohen, L. P. 1990. "Hard Time." *Wall Street Journal.* December 18: A1.

Cohen, L. E. & M. Felson. 1979. "Social Change and Crime Rate Trends: A Routine Activities Approach." *American Sociological Review* 44:588–608.

Coleman, D. 1996. "The Lock 'Em Up Judge Facing Prison Himself." *New Jersey Lawyer.* December 9:1.

Coleman, J. W. 1992. "The Theory of White-Collar Crime from Sutherland to the 1990s." In *White-Collar Crime Reconsidered,* edited by K. Schlegel & D. Weisburd. Boston, MA: Northeastern Press.

Coleman, J. 1994. *Criminal Elite.* New York: St. Martin's Press.

Collins, J. & F. Schmidt. 1993. "Personality, Integrity, and White-Collar Crime." Personnel Psychology. 46:295–311.

Conlan, M. F. 1991. "Con Man Reveals White-Collar Crime Secrets to R.Phs." *Drug Topics,* 135(23):55.

Conley, J. 2000. "Knocking the Starch Out of White-collar Crime." *Risk Management* 47(11):14–22.

Corporate Crime Reporter. 2000. "Interview with Allen Ellis." March 6. Available online at www.corporatecrimereporter.com. Accessed July 15, 2001.

Corwin, J. & B. McCormick. 1999. "Students Look for Ethics in Criminal Behavior." *Baylor Business Review* 17(2):10–11.

Council, J. 1997. "Dallas Solo Fights Charges in Federal Retrial." *Texas Lawyer.* September 15:1.

Coughlin, K. 1994. "Ex-Inmate Advises Priore." *Star Ledger.* October 6.

Covington, J. 1984. "Insulation from Labeling." *Criminology* 22:619–643.

Crable, A. 1995. "This Trail Crew's Pros and Cons." *Backpacker* 23(9):15.

Cressey, D. R. 1953. *Other People's Money.* Glencoe, IL: Free Press.

Crime in the United States. 2001. Washington, DC: USGPO, U.S. Department of Justice.

Crouch, B. 1993. "Is Incarceration Really Worse?" *Justice Quarterly* 10:67–88.

Cullen, F., Mathers, R. A., Clark, G. A., & J. B. Cullen. 1983. "Public Support for Punishing White-Collar Crime." *Journal of Criminal Justice* 11:481–493.

Cullen, F. Clark, G. A., Cullen, J. B., & R. A. Mathers. 1985. "Attribution, Salience, and Attitudes towards Criminal Sanctioning." *Criminal Justice and Behavior* 12:305–331.

Cutter, K. 2001. "The Professional." *W* 30(3):194–196.

Czunder, G. & R. Mueller. 1987. "The Role of Guilt and It's Implication in the Treatment of Criminals." *International Journal of Offender Therapy and Comparative Criminology* 31:61–70.

Dabney, D. 1995. "Neutralization and Deviance in the Workplace." *Deviant Behavior* 16:313–333.

Daily Telegraph. 1992. "Ex-Mayor in 'Jail-Sex' Row." January 6:3.

Dallao, M. 1996. "Fighting Prison Rape." *Corrections Today* 58(7):100–104.

Daly, M. 1989. "Gender and Varieties of White–Collar Crime." *Criminology,* 27:769–793.

Davis, K. & E. Burt. 2001. "Anatomy of a Fraud." *Kiplinger's Personal Finance Magazine* 55(3):88–93.

Doege, D. 2001. "Former Funeral Home Worker Charged in Fraud." *Milwaukee Journal Sentinel.* January 24:03B.

Dolinko, D. 2000. "Justice in the Age of Sentencing Guidelines." *Ethics* 110: 563–580.

Douthat, S. 1989. "Federal Prison Camp–Houses Powerful White-Collar Criminals among Guests at Club Fed." *Los Angeles Times* April 23:14.

Eichenwald, K. 2002. White-Collar Defense Stance. *The New York Times.* March 3:3

Eitle, D. J. 2000. "Regulatory Justice." *Justice Quarterly.* 17:809–835.

Ettore, B. 1994. "Nobody Put Me in Prison But Myself." *Management Review.* 83(5): 14–15.

Ewinger, J. 1995. "Prosecutors Seek to Have Doctor Who Embezzled Returned to Prison." *Plain Dealer.* December 1:1B.

Fahrenkopf, F. J. 1997. "Letter to the Editor." *Bloomberg Magazine.* Available online at. Accessed July 7, 2001.

Farnham, A. 1990. "The Savings and Loan Felons." *Fortune* 122(12):90–105.

Fels, A. 2001. "Jail Would Hurt More Than Fines." *Canbury Times.* July 5:11.

Felson, M. 1998. *Crime and Everyday Life.* 2 ed. Thousand Oaks, CA: Pine Forge Press.

Final Report of the Task Force on Gambling Addiction in Maryland. 1990. Baltimore, MD: Department of Health and Mental Hygiene.

Flannery, P. 1998. "He Has to Forget Himself–Ex-Inmate Offers Jail Advice for Ex-Governor." *Arizona Republic.* February 3:A7.

Fleckenstein, M. P. & J. C. Bowers. 2000. "When Trust is Betrayed." *Journal of Business Ethics.* 23: 111–115.

Foy, N. 1995. "New Home Much Like Old." *San Antonio Express.* June 3:1B.

Franzen, R. 2001. "Embezzler Doesn't Jump to Make Food." *Oregonian.* Fecruary 19:C5.

Frayler, M. 2000. "A Busted Broker Tells of a Stretch in the Big House." *New York Post.* May 22:49.

Freeman, R. 2000. *Popular Culture and Corrections.* Lanham, MD: American Correctional Association.

Friedman, M. 1998. "Coping with Consumer Fraud." *Journal of Consumer Affairs* 32:1–11.

Friedrichs, D. 1996. *Trusted Criminals: White-collar Crime in Contemporary Society.* Belmont, CA: Wadsworth.

Fuquay, J. 2000. "Irving Broker Gets Five Year Term–Church Members Targeted in Scam." *Fort Worth Star-Telegram.* January 8:3.

Furfaro, D. T. 2001. "Rexford, NY, Man Sentenced to Prison for Financial Crimes." *Knight-Ridder Business News.* March 2.

Gallagher, E. 1990. "Emotional, Social, and Physical Health Characteristics of Older Men in Prison." *International Journal of Aging and Human Development* 31:251–265.

Galvin, A. 2000. "Defiant Swindler Gets 30 Year Sentence." *Bloomburg News.* April 29:2.

Ganey, T. 1994. "Webster Reports to Prison–It's Not Club Fed." *St. Louis Dispatch.* February 19:01A.

Ganzini, L., McFarland, B., & J. Bloom. 1990. "Victims of Fraud." *Bulletin of the American Academy of Psychiatry Law* 18:55–63.

Garland, G. 2000. "An Inmate Primer for Life Behind Bars." *Baltimore Sun.* December 17: 2F.

Geis, G. 1996. "Base on Balls for White-Collar Crime." In *Three Strikes and You're Out–Vengeance as Public Policy*, edited by D. Shichor & D. Sechrest. Thousand Oaks, CA: Sage.

Geis, G. 2000. "On the Absence of Self-Control as the Basis for a General Theory of Crime." *Theoretical Criminology* 4:35–53.

Gerber, J. 1994. "Club Fed in Japan?" *International Journal of Offender Therapy and Comparative Criminology.* 38:163–174.

Gest, T. 1985. "Are White-Collar Crooks Getting Off Too Easy?" *U.S. News and World Report.* July 1:43.

Gibson, K. 2000. "Excuses, Excuses: Moral Slippage in the Workplace." *Business Horizons.* 43:65–85.

Gillies, J. 2000. "The Great Escape." In *Chicken Soup for the Prisoner's Soul*, edited by J. Canfield, M. Hansen, & T. Lagana. Deerfield Beach, FL: Health Communications.

Gladwin, B. 1999. "Employee/Inmate Relations." In *A View from the Trenches: A Manual for Wardens by Wardens.* Lanham, MD: American Correctional Association.

Glasberg, D. S. & D. Skidmore. 1998. "The Dialectics of White-Collar Crime." *The American Journal of Economics and Society.* 57:423–446.

Goffman, E. 1959. *The Presentation of Self in Everyday Life.* New York: Doubleday.

Goffman, 1963. *Stigma: Notes on the Management of a Spoiled Identity.* Englewood Cliffs, NJ: Prentice Hall.

Goldman, L. 2001. "Club Fed." *Forbes.* February 5:204.

Gondles, J. A. 1998. "Influencing Public Perception." *Corrections Today* 60:6.

Gottfredson, M. & T. Hirschi. 1990. *A General Theory of Crime.* Stanford, CA: Stanford University Press.

Grasmick, H. G., Tittle, C. R., Bursik, R. J. Jr., & B. J. Arneklev. 1993. "Testing the Core Empirical Implications of Gottfredson and Hirschi's General Theory of Crime." *Journal of Research in Crime and Delinquency* 30:5–29.

Gray, R. 1997. "Clamping Down on Worker Crime." *Nation's Business* 85:44–45.

Green, G. 1997. *Occupational Crime.* 2 ed. Belmont, CA: Wadsworth.

Greenwald, J. 1990. "A Stiff Term for the Wizard." *Time* 136(2):82–83.

Hagan, J. & A. Palloni. 1986. "Club Fed and the Sentencing of White-Collar Offenders before and After Watergate." *Criminology* 24:603–622.

Hall, B. 1989. "Disgraced Speculator Pays Dues at Club Fed." *Courier Journal.* November 14:02A.

Hamlin, J. E. 1988. "The Misplaced Role of Rational Choice in Neutralization Theory." *Criminology* 26(3):425–438.

Hansen, S. 2000. "Taking Money Was Easier than I Thought." *Good Housekeeping* 230(4):99–104.

Harper's. 1999. "Reach Out and Whack Someone." 2999(795):29.

Harrington, S. J. 1996. "The Effects of Codes of Ethics and Personal Denial of Responsibility on Computer Abuse Judgements and Intentions." *MIS Quarterly* 20(3):257–278.

Harris, D. K. & M. Benson. 1999. "Theft in Nursing Homes: An Overlooked form of Abuse." *Journal of Elder Abuse & Neglect* 11:73–90.

Hawk, K.M. 1994. "Corrections Must Take Action Using Courage, Creativity, and Leadership." *Corrections Today* 56:72–73.

Henderson, J. 2001. "Pros at Being Cons Help Clients Adjust to Prison Life." *Houston Chronicle.* September 24:1.

Henry, J. and G. S. Odiorme, 1989. "Eleven Myths about Hiring Ex-offenders." *Personnel.* 66:27–29.

Higgins, M. 1999. "Sizing Up Sentences." *ABA Journal* 85:42–47.

Hirschi, T. 1969. *Causes of Delinquency.* Berkley, CA: University of Berkley Press.

Hirschi, T. & M. Gottfredson. 1987. "Causes of White-Collar Crime." *Criminology* 25(4):949–972.

Holding, R. & W. Carlsen. 1999. "Hollow Words: Federal Prosecutors Say White-Collar Crime is a Priority." *San Francisco Chronicle.* November 16:A1.

Holland, J. 2000. "Former Sumter Football Coach is Sentenced to 90 Days in Jail." *Associate Press Newswire.* May 19.

Hollinger, R. C. 1991. "Neutralizing in the Workplace." *Deviant Behavior* 12:169–202.

Houston Chronicle. 1985. "Jake Butcher Gets 20-year Sentence." June 4:3.

Insurance Fraud Bureau of Massachusetts. 2000. *2000 IFB Annual Report.* Boston, MA: IFB. Available online at www.ifb.org. Accessed June 200, 2001.

Jacobs, P. 1998. "Club Fed? Women's Prison in Dublin Has Some Perks, But It's No Picnic." *San Francisco Chronicle.* June 6:A15.

Janhevich, D. E. 1998. *Changing Nature of Fraud in Canada.* Ottawa, Ontario: Canadian Center on Justice Statistics.

Jenkins, L. 2002. "Slap on Wrist Seems Par." *San Diego Union-Tribune.* March 2:nc2

Jesilow, P., Pontell, H., and G. Geis. 1993. *Prescription for Profit.* Berkeley: University of California Press.

Johnston, R. 2002 "The Battle against White-Collar Crime." *USA Today Magazine.* 130(2680):36-38

Kaczor, B. 1999. "Johnson Begins two-year Prison Sentence." *Associated Press Newswires.* August 30.

Kappeler, V. (1996). *The Mythology of Crime and Criminal Justice.* Prospect Heights, IL: Waveland.

Keenan, C. E., Brown, G. C., Pontell, H. N., & G. Geis. 1985. "Medical Student's Attitudes on Physician Fraud and Abuse." *Journal of Medical Education* 60: 167–173.

Keller, S. 2000. "Time-Out." In *Chicken Soup for the Prisoner's Soul,* edited by J. Canfield, M. Hansen, & T. Lagana. Deerfield Beach, FL: Health Communications.

Kircher, R. 1997. "Mind of an Embezzler." *Business Journal-Milwaukee.* October 17:1–2.

Kisken, T. 1999. "Convicts Teach Ethics Students." *Wall Street Journal.* Available online at www.wsj.com. Accessed July 7, 2001.

Klein, A. 1996. "A Thief So Smart, So Stupid." *Baltimore Sun.* May 19:1D.

Knapp, E. 1996. "Life In Prison." *Letters From Prison.* Available online at. Accessed May 15, 2001.

Knox, D. 1999. "White-Collar Crime Not Exactly Hard Time." *Denver Post* March 11:C01.

Koepp, S. 1988. "Fraud, Fraud, Fraud." *Time.* August 15:28–29.

Krueger, J. 1999. "Quiet Crimes: White-collar Theft on the Rise." *Orlando Business Journal* 16(24): 1–3.

Kubler-Ross, E. 1970. *On Death and Dying.* New York: Scribner.

Larsen, D. 1989. "Make Crime Pay." *Los Angeles Times.* May 8:1.

Lasley, J. P. 1988. "Toward a Control Theory of White-Collar Offending." *Journal of Quantitative Criminology* 4(4):347–362.

Levin, S. 1990. "Serving the Community Instead of Serving Time." *Dallas Morning News.* July 11:1C.

Loane, S. 2000. "White-Collar Criminals Suffer a Bad Case of Jailhouse Blues." *Sydney Morning Herald.* December 11:24.

Locy, T. 1998. "The Nicest People . . . Do This Kind of Stuff." *The Washington Post.* October 1:A12.

Lodge, B. 2001. "Man Gets 23-Year Term for Defrauding Elderly: Officials Say Penalty Uncommon for White-Collar Crime." *Dallas Morning News.* May 18:38A.

Lore, D. 1992. "Minimum Security, Maximum Cost." *Columbus Dispatch.* September 6:1F.

Lott, J. R. 1990. "Getting Tough on White-collar Crime." *Regulation* 13(1):18–19.

Maakestad, W. J. 1991. "Doing Time for Safety Violations." *Orange County Business Journal.* March 4:A1–A4.

Maddocks, P. M. 1992. "Victimization and White-Collar Crime." *Management Accounting* 73:16.

Mann, K., Wheeler, S., & A. Sarat. 1980. "Sentencing of White-collar Criminals." *American Criminal Law Review.* 17(4):409–520.

Marshall, T. 1993. "Book on the Pens is Tops, Bar None." *Houston Chronicle.* July 14:21.

Martin, R., Mutchnick, R. & W. T. Austin. 1990. *Pioneers in Criminological Thought.* New York: MacMillan.

Matza, D. 1964. Delinquency and Drift. New York: Wiley.

Mazure, C. M., Bruce, M. L., Maciejewski, P., & S. C. Jacobs. 2000. "Adverse Life Events and Cognitive Personality Characteristics in the Prediction of Major Depression and Antidepressant Response." *American Journal of Psychiatry* 157(6):896–903.

McCaghy, C. 1968. "Drinking and Deviance Disavowed." *Social Problems.* 16:43–49.

McAllister, B. 1999. "Lobbyist Sentenced to Prison for Fraud." *Denver Post.* October 26:B01.

McCarthy, C. 1996. "Judge Gets His Own Medicine." *National Catholic Reporter* 32(25):13.

Merton, R. 1938. "Social Structure and Anomie." *American Sociological Review* 3:672–682.

Messner, S. and R. Rosenfeld. 2001. *Crime and the American Dream.* 2 ed. Belmont, CA: Wadsworth.

Miller, G. 1993. "White-Collar Criminals Share One Trait–Greed." *Corrections Today.* 55(3):22–23.

Miller, R. 1996. "Program Puts Inmates to Work as VA Volunteers." *Dallas Morning News.* September 15:2H.

Minor, W. W. 1981. "Techniques of Neutralization." *Journal of Research in Crime and Delinquency* 18:295–318.

Mize, J. 2001. "Former Federal Inmates Offer Advice to Soon-to-be Prisoners." *Associated Press Newswires.* March 17.

Modic, R. 2001. "Judge Sentences Chari to Eight Years." *Dayton Daily News.* July 11:1A.

Mokhiber, R. 1988. *Corporate Crime and Violence.* San Francisco, CA: Sierra Club.

Mokhiber, R. 2000. "White-Collar Crime Spree." *Multinational Monitor.* August:38.

Moore, E. & M. Mills. 1990. "The Neglected Victims and Unexamined Costs of White-Collar Crime." *Crime and Delinquency* 36(3):408–418.

Morvillo, R. G. 1999. "Mandatory Restitution." *New York Law Review* August 3: 3–10.

Moss, D. 1995. "Charity Embezzler Gets 7-Year Sentence." *USA Today.* June 23:3A.

Nachtigal, J. 1998. "Former Arizona Governor Sentenced to 2 1/2 Years in Prison." *Associated Press Newswires.*

Nadler, P. S. 1992. "Life in Banker's Jail: No Club Fed." *American Banker.* November 30:4.

Nadler, P. S. 2000. "White-Collar Crime and Punishment." *The Secured Lender.* 56:16–20.

Nash, K. S. 1998. "From Pros to Cons." *Computer World. October 19:101.*

News Gazette Champaign. 2001. "Shop Till You Drop." May 29:A6.

New York Times. 1995. "Inmate Beats Ex-Trooper Who Faked Prints." March 23:B9.

Nicholson, L. J., Shebar, T. F., & M. R. Weinberg. 2000. "Computer Crimes." *American Criminal Law Review* 37(2):207–267.

Nowlin, S. 2001. "San Antonio Man Remains In Jail on Financial Fraud Charges." *Knight-Ridder Tribune Business News.* February 16.

O'Donnell, M. 1992. "Sentencing Examples." *Chicago Sun Times.* October 11:42.

O'Toole, F. 1996. "Hazards of the Sentencing Guidelines." *The CRA Journal* 66(2): 36-39.

Omaha World Herald. 1999. "Program Helps Former Felons Dive Into Labor Pool." November 21:28G.

Otter, A. 1985. "Mounting Charges of Leniency." *Wall Street Journal.* October 30.

Pankratz, H. 2000. "Hockey Mom Gets Ten Year Sentence." *Denver Post.* July 18:B02.

Payne, B. K. 1998. "Conceptualizing the Impact of Health Care Crimes on the Poor." *Free Inquiry in Creative Sociology* 26:159–168.

Payne, B.K. 2000. *Crime and Elder Abuse.* Springfield, IL: Charles C Thomas.

Payne, B. K. & R. R. Gainey. 1998. "A Qualitative Assessment of the Pains Experienced on Electronic Monitoring." *International Journal of Offender Therapy and Comparative Criminology* 42(2):149–163.

Payne, B. K. & R. R. Gainey. 2001. *Family Violence and Criminal Justice: A Life Course Approach.* Cincinnati, OH: Anderson Publishing.

Payne, B.K. and E. Stevens. 1999 "An Examination of Sanchions Imposed on Alabama Lawyers." *Justice Professional* 12:17-43.

People Weekly. 2000. "Object Lessons: CEOs in the Slammer?" October 30:95.

Pilegi, N. 1986. "Wiseguy: Life in a Mafia Family." *Houston Chronicle.* April 22:2.

Pollack, H. & Smith, A. B. 1983. "White-Collar Versus Street Crime: Sentencing Disparity." *Judicature* 4:174–182.

Pollick, M. 1998. "Downtime: Life At Prison Camp." *Sarasota Herald Tribune.* August 15:1A.

Pollock, N. L. & J. M. Hashmall. 1991. "The Excuses of Child Molesters." *Behavioral Sciences and the Law* 9:53–59.

Pontell, H., Jesilow, P., & G. Geis. 1982. "Policing Physicians: Practitioner Fraud and Abuse in a Government Medical Program." *Social Problems* 30:117–126.

Pontell, H. N., Jesilow, P., & G. Geis. 1984. "Practitioner Fraud and Abuse in Medical Benefits Programs." *Law and Policy* 4:405–424.

Pontell, H. N. & A. Frid. 2000. "International Financial Fraud: Emerging Trends and Issues." In *International Criminal Justice: Issues in Global Perspective,* edited by D. Rounds. Boston, MA: Allyn and Bacon.

Posner, R. 1980. "Optimal Sentencing of White-Collar Offenders." *American Criminal Law Review* 17:409–480.

Poveda, T. 1994. *Rethinking White-Collar Crime.* Westport, CT: Greenwood.

Pratt, T. C. & F. Cullen. 2000. "The Empirical Status of Gottfredson and Hirschi's General Theory of Crime." *Criminology* 38:931–962.

Psychology Today. 1997. "Judge Not." 10(4):28–31.

Quevedo, E. L. 1992. "Effective Environmental Program Could Keep Executives out of Jail." *The Business Journal* 10:24–25.

Quinn, M. J. & S. Tomita. 1997. *Elder Abuse.* New York: Springer.

Rackmill, S. 1992. "Understanding and Sanctioning the White-Collar Offender." *Federal Probation.* 56:26–33.

Reason, T. 2000. "Jailhouse Shock." CFO, *The Magazine for Senior Financial Executives* 16:111–118.

Reed, G. & P. Yeager. 1996. "Organizational Offending and Neoclassical Criminology." *Criminology* 34:353–382.

Reguly, R. 1992. "When Pros Become Cons." *Canadian Business* 65:107–111.

Reilly, R. 1998. "Need an Excuse? Take it from the Pros. (Excuses Used by Pro Athletes after Getting in Trouble)." *Sports Illustrated.* March 16:134.

Ress, D. 2001. "New Jersey's Insurance Fraud Office Reports on 2000 Cases." *Knight-Ridder/Tribune Business News.* March 2.

Reuters. 2000. "Prison Caterer Gets Taste of Own Cuisine." August 8 Available online at.

Rivera, R. 1998. "Orem, Utah, Lawyer Sentenced for Duping Thousands." *Knight Ridder/Tribune Business News.* Novermber 10.

Roberts, M. 2000. "Embezzlers Beware." *Portland Oregonian.* March 12:A01.

Robertson, J. 1999. "Cruel and Unusual Punishment in United States Prisons." *American Criminal Law Review* 3645:1-45

Roehrich, C. 1998. "Restorative Justice: A Correctional Institution's Approach." In *Best Practices: Excellence in Corrections,* edited by E. E. Rhine. Lanham, MD: American Correctional Association.

Roig-Franzia, M. 2000. "Retirement Prison." *New Orleans Picayne.* July 23:A01

Rokach, A. & J. Cripps. 1999. "Incarcerated Men and Their Perceived Sources of Their Loneliness." *International Journal of Offender Therapy and Comparative Criminology* 43:78–89.

Rolls, M. 1998. "Can the One Man Crime Wave Be Stopped?" *Business Credit* 98(7):24.

Rosoff, S., Pontell, H. N., & R. Tillman. 1998 *Profit Without Honor: White-Collar Crime and the Looting of America.* Upper Saddle River, NJ: Prentice Hall.

Ruth, R. 2000. "Swindler's Victims Speak Out." *Columbus Dispatch.* August 10:1C.

Sampson, R. J. & J. H. Laub. 1993. *Crime in the Making: Pathways and Turning Points Through Life.* Cambridge, MA: Harvard University Press.

Sandrik, K. 1993. "Ethical Misconduct in Healthcare." *Healthcare Financial Management.* 47:35–42.

Sangree, H. and H. Becerra. 1999. "Sentenced to Service." *Los Angeles Times.* December 3:B2.

Saum, C. A., Surratt, H. L., Inciardi, J. A. & R. E. Bennett. 1995. "Sex in Prison." *Prison Journal* 75:413–430.

Sayre, A. 1998. "Examiners Say Workplace Fraud is on the Rise." *Marketing News.* 32(1):22.

Saxe, F. 2000. "Out of Prison and Back on the Airwaves." *Billboard* 1112:93.

Schill, R. & D. Marcus. 1998. "Incarceration and Learned Helplessness." *International Journal of Offender Therapy and Comparative Criminology* 42:224–232.

Schlegel, K. & D. Weisburd. 1992. (Eds.). *White-Collar Crime Reconsidered.* Boston, MA: Northeastern University Press.

Schroeder, M. & A. Barrett. 1996. "A Bigger Stick against Insider Traders." *Business Week.* May 27:34–35.

Sciacca, J. 1997."The Agony of Club Fed." *Boston Herald.* May:15.

Scott, M. B. & S. Lyman. 1968. "Accounts" *American Sociological Review* 33:46–62.

Semerad, T. 1998. "The New Waldholtz." *The Salt Lake Tribune.* June 11:A1.

Serwer, A. 2000. "Guys You Wouldn't Want as Your Broker." *Fortune* 141(6):56–58.

Seymour, A. 1998. "Restorative Justice in Prison." *In A View from the Trenches,* Edited by E. Rhine. Lanham, MD: American Correctional Association.

Sheley, J. 1980. "Is Neutralization Necessary for Criminal Behavior?" *Deviant Behavior* 2:49–72.

Shover, N., G. L. Fox, & M. Mills. 1998. "Long Term Consequences of Victimization by White-Collar Crime." *Justice Quarterly* 11:75–90.

Simon, D. R. & F. E. Hagan. 1999. *White-Collar Deviance.* Boston, MA: Allyn & Bacon.

Smith, A. B. & L. Berlin. 1981. *Treating the Criminal Offender.* Englewood Cliffs, NJ: Prentice Hall.

Solomon, J. 1998. "Watching Mike." *Newsweek* 131(9): 54–55.

Soothill, K., B. Francis, & E. Ackerly. 1997. *British Journal of Criminology* 37:582–592.

Steurer, S. 1998. "The Correctional Education Program: Peer Tutoring." In B*est Practices: Excellence in Corrections,* edited by E. Rhine. Lanham, MD: American Correctional Association.

Sutherland, E. 1939. *Principles of Criminology.* 3rd ed. Philadelphia: Lippincott.

Sutherland, E. 1940. "White-collar Criminality." *American Sociological Review.* 5:1–12.

Sutherland, E. 1983. *White-Collar Crime: The Uncut Version.* New Haven, CT: Yale University Press.

Swanson, W. 2001. "The Doctor is In." *St. Paul's Magazine* 29:68–72.

Sykes, G. & D. Matza. 1957. "Techniques of Neutralization." *American Sociological Review* 22:664–670.

Sykes, G. 1958. *The Society of Captives.* Princeton, NJ: Princeton University Press.

Szockyj, E. & N. Frank. 1996. (Eds.) "Introduction." In *Corporate Victimization of Women,* edited by E. Szockyj & N. Frank. Boston, MA: Northeastern University Press.

Tata, J. 2000. "She Said, He Said." *Journal of Management* 26:1133.

Taylor, A. M. 1990. "CEOs in the Slammer or What to Do While Your Boss Does Time." *Communication World.* 7(6): 156–162.

Tayoun, 2000. *Going to Prison.* 4th ed. Brunswick, ME: Biddle Publishing.

TerMeer, R. 1997. "The White-Collar Criminal's Survivor Guide." *Harper's* 294:19–20.

The Economist. 2001. "Coming to a Neighborhood Near You." May 5:1.

Thompson, T. 1991. "Attorneys Find it Harder to Get Clients into Club Fed." *Knight Ridder/Tribune Business Review.* December 22:6.

Touby, L.1994. "In the Company of Thieves." *Journal of Business Strategy* 15(3):24–31.

Trends in Community Supervision of Offenders. 1997. Washington, DC: USGPO, U.S. General Accounting Office.

Turner, D. L. & R. G. Stephenson. 1993. "The Lure of White-Collar Crime." *Security Management* 37:57–58.

Van Alphen, T. 2001. "Toronto Stock Promoter Gets Seven Years." *Toronto Star.* January 27:B11.

Vaughan, D. 1983. *Controlling Unlawful Organizational Behavior.* Chicago: University of Chicago Press.

Vaughan, D. 1992. "The Micro-Macro Connection in White-Collar Theory." In *White-Collar Crime Reconsidered,* edited by K. Schlegel & D. Weisburd. Boston, MA: Northeastern University Press.

Waga, P. 1991. "Hard Times at Federal Prison." *Gannett News Service.* April 8.

Washington Post. 1989. "Is Grass Greener at Club Fed?" August 31:03.

Weisburd, D., Chayet, E., & E. J. Waring. 1990. "White-collar Crime and Criminal Careers." *Crime and Delinquency.* 36(3):342–255.

Weisburd, D. & E. J. Waring. (with E. Chayet), 2001. *White-Collar Crime and Criminal Careers.* Cambridge, UK: Cambridge University Press.

Weisburd, D., Waring, E., and E. Chayet. 1995. "Specific Deterrence in a Sample of Offenders Convicted of White-Collar Crime." *Criminology* 33:587–596.

Weisburd, D., Waring, E., Chayet, E., Dickman, D., Fisher, R. M., & S. Plant. 1991. *White-Collar Crime and Criminal Careers.* Washington, DC: USGPO, National Institute of Justice.

Weisburd, D., Waring, E. Chayet, E., Dickman, D., Fisher, R. M., & S. Plant. 1993. *White-Collar Crime and Criminal Careers.* Washington, DC: USGPO, National Institute of Justice, U.S. Department of Justice.

Wells, J. T. 1990. "Six Myths About Fraud." *Journal of Accounting* 169:82–86.

Wheeler, S. 1992. "The Problem with Motivation." In *White-Collar Crime Reconsidered,* edited by K. Schlegel & D. Weisburd. Boston, MA: Northeastern University Press.

Wheeler, S., Mann, K., & Sarat, A.1988a. *Sitting In Judgment.* New Haven, CT: Yale University Press.

Wheeler, S., Weisburd, S., Waring, E., & N. Bode. 1988b. "White-Collar Crimes and Criminals." *American Criminal Law Review* 25:331–359.

Wilkie, D. 1990. "Club Fed Prison Holds Key to Punishment of the Privileged." *San Diego Union Tribune.* August 25:A1.

Will, S., H. N. Pontell, & R. Cheung. 1998. "Risky Business Revisited." *Crime and Delinquency* 44:367–386.

Wilson, S. 1998. "Symington Needs Community Service After Prison." *Arizona Republic.* February 1:A2.

Winn, M. E. 1996. "The Strategic and Systematic Management of Denial in the Cognitive/Behavioral Treatment of Sexual Offenders." *Sexual Abuse: A Journal of Research and Treatment* 8:25–36.

Wooldredge, J. 1994. "Crime and Victimization in a Southwest Correctional Facility." *Journal of Criminal Justice* 22:367–381.

Wright, G. L. 2001. "Matthews, N.C., Executive to Plead Guilty." *Knight Ridder/Tribune Business News.* March 15: 01.

Wright, J. P. & F. Cullen. 2000. "Juvenile Involvement in Occupational Delinquency." *Criminology* 38:863–896.

WVSOM Magazine. 2001. "Doing Time." Available online at. Accessed July 14, 2001.

Yu, S. 1998. "Computer Fraud." *Review of Business.* 20:22.

Zeune, G. D. 2000. "Are You Teaching Your Employees to Steal?" *Strategic Finance* 82:34–40.

Zimbardo, P. 1971. "The Power and Pathology of Imprisonment." *Congressional Record/* (Serial No. 15, October 25, 1971). Hearings before subcommittee Number 3 of the Committee on the Judiciary, House of Representatives, Ninety-Second Congress.

NAME INDEX

159

SUBJECT INDEX